J.S. Bach's *The Art of Fugue*

J.S. Bach's *The Art of Fugue*

THE WORK AND ITS INTERPRETATION

Hans Heinrich Eggebrecht

English Translation by Jeffrey L. Prater

Iowa State University Press / Ames

Authorization to photocopy items for internal or personal use, or the internal or personal use of specific clients, is granted by Iowa State University Press, provided that the base fee of $.10 per copy is paid directly to the copyright Clearance Center, 27 Congress Street, Salem MA 01970. For those organizations that have been granted a photocopy licence by CCC, a separate system of payments has been arranged. The fee codes for users of the Transactional Reporting Service are 0-8138-1489-8 $.10.

∞ Printed on acid-free paper in the United States of America

First edition, 1993

Library of Congress Cataloging-in-Publication Data

Eggebrecht, Hans Heinrich.
  [Bachs Kunst der Fuge. English]
  J. S. Bach's The art of fugue: the work and its interpretation
Hans Heinrich Eggebrecht: English translation by Jeffrey L. Prater.
  —1st ed.
    p.   cm.
  Includes bibliographical references and index.
  ISBN 0-8138-1489-8 (acid-free paper)
  1. Bach, Johann Sebastian, 1685-1750. Kunst der Fuge. I. Title.
II. Title: J.S. Bach's The art of fugue.
MT145.B14E4513 1993
786' . 1872—dc20   93-1281

                                                                                MN

CONTENTS

ABOUT THIS BOOK

From the German Edition

In this text, Hans Heinrich Eggebrecht develops a new interpretation of J.S. Bach's *The Art of Fugue,* based on a profound knowledge of Baroque-era thought and intense score study. Starting with the work's celebrated BACH theme, Eggebrecht attempts to show that *The Art of Fugue* contains an assertion of the composer's deeply held faith, and that aspects of Bach's spiritual convictions permeate the entire musical fabric of the work. Eggebrecht postulates that *The Art of Fugue* is actually a musical representation of Bach's beliefs about the God-human relationship, and argues that the Christian doctrine of "salvation by grace" is the core concept that provides the work with its expressive content in much the same way that the opening ground-theme subject acts as a basic generating source for all subsequent musical materials.

Although *The Art of Fugue* is regarded by the musical world as one of the most significant examples of Bach's contrapuntal craft, the author convincingly argues that this work has an important spiritual dimension that goes beyond considerations of the composer's craftsmanship. Eggebrecht devotes this book to a lively and controversial discussion of unprovable matters; that is, to those aspects of expressive content which he believes are concealed both within and behind the musical materials.

TRANSLATOR'S FOREWORD

Why should a person who has spent nearly his entire musical career as a composer and theorist take considerable time away from those endeavors to translate a work of musicological criticism? In fact, from my perspective near the end of this task, I can provide neither a single nor simple answer to this question. Nevertheless, the question is vital to my personal involvement in the project, and I shall devote this foreword to some of the motivational stimuli and ideas that seemed (and still seem) important reasons for bringing Eggebrecht's study into English.

The clean and architectonic music of J.S. Bach has captivated me since childhood. I clearly remember in the mid 1950s (about age eight) when my father bought our first long-playing stereophonic record player. Along with the wonder of early demonstration records with titles like "This is Stereo!" came an ever increasing flood of LP's into the house. Our record cabinet began to bulge, then overflow, with frequent stops at record stores. My mother even bought a complete set of "musical masterpieces" at the local supermarket, one record per week out of her grocery budget. It is from this set of "budget classics," where all the artists, conductors and ensembles remained cloaked in anonymity (probably for good reason), that I remember hearing Bach for the first time— the D-minor Concerto for two violins (BWV 1043). I completely wore out the grooves of that heavy black disk by playing it over and over, while pretending to be a great conductor. There were other composers represented in that set (and still others not represented in the set) who I would come to understand and greatly admire with time, but as a child and then a young teen, I fell in love with the preludes, fugues, and concerti of that great German master. At that time my "classical music" world was, for good or ill, mostly Bach.

Following were years of piano lessons complete with Bach Inventions, Sinfonias, and the *Well-Tempered Clavier*. My first attempt at composition took place in early high school and was a piece that almost resembled a Bach two-part invention. Like most university music students, I analyzed and wrote countless four-voice chorales and then went on to Bach counterpoint and fugue. Despite the reams of music paper containing exercises and compositions "in the style of," and the obligatory reading of numerous technical and sometimes painfully dull theoretical and historical studies, I never lost my love for the music of J.S. Bach. Even after years of developing a taste for and concentrating almost exclusively on more contemporary musical idioms, I still regularly return to the musical roots of my childhood. During these times, I frequently listen to, play, and study the music of J.S. Bach, and in doing so, I am often refreshed and musically reinspired. There is no doubt that this lifelong passion for Bach's music has provided at least some small predisposition for my interest in the project at hand.

I cannot precisely recall when I first learned of *The Art of Fugue*, but it was immediately after a brilliantly played recital by my colleague, organist Lynn Zeigler, that I too came to think of this work, in the words of Alban Berg, as "deepest music!!"[1] A year or so later, I began analyzing *The Art of Fugue* in preparation for several lectures during the "Bach year" (1985). It was during this period of study that I began reading and collecting books about the work and obtaining various editions of the score. In spring of that year, I had the opportunity to travel to Europe, and while in Berlin and Vienna, I purchased copies of Eggebrecht's book and the published facsimiles of Bach's autograph and the first printing of *The Art of Fugue*.

Though Eggebrecht's erudite German was not easy reading, I was immediately taken by his innovative interpretation of the well-known (one might even say well-worn) "B-A-C-H motto." Eggebrecht's investigation of the entire third subject of the quadruple fugue (not just the "B-A-C-H" front end) is both refreshing and analytically sensible. I am aware of no other study of *The Art of Fugue* which treats the double discant clausula at the end of this subject as anything more than a barely necessary appendix to the composer's clearly inscribed surname. It is as though the instantaneous clarity of the first four pitches had, until Eggebrecht, completely eclipsed the importance of the remaining pitches. This is ironic, since musicians for generations have been taught that fugue subjects are musical *monads*. Whether the decision to look at the subject as a whole prompted Eggebrecht's interpretation of the work, or whether his theory prompted him to study the entire subject, the concept of placing additional emphasis on the double discant clausula was the key that opened up the wider possibilities of his interpretation. From this simple change in perspective, coupled with the author's command of Baroque rhetorical figures and his knowledge of analytical studies, the rest of the book seemed to follow almost effortlessly.

This is not to say that his view concerning Bach's intended meaning in *The Art of Fugue* is uncontroversial. Indeed, Eggebrecht is keenly aware that there are those who will take issue with him "on the grounds that they [the ideas he

---

[1] See chapter 10, p.125.

introduces] present an ideologically corrupted analysis of Bach's intentions."[2] Certainly, all readers will not equally embrace the position that Bach intended to express aspects of the Christian doctrine of "salvation by grace" in *The Art of Fugue*. For his part, however, Eggebrecht is careful to reiterate time and again that this assertion can never be proved and that he only intends to build a position worthy of debate.

Eggebrecht's study has a number of enthusiastic supporters, however. In a major review, Hermann Conen begins by mildly chiding Eggebrecht for the reticence he shows in his preface, then proceeds to strongly advocate both Eggebrecht's methodology and conclusions:

> This interpretation, which Eggebrecht himself knows 'seldom ventures' out into our modern world," is not just an esoteric argument, but rather, develops from a clear analysis of the musical materials and their position within the work. The result is a synopsis of everything that one can reliably say about meaning in Bach's compositions.[3]

Though not as certain as Conen about the author's conclusions, Wilfried Gruhn also endorses Eggebrecht's approach:

> Even if one does not always agree with his [Eggebrecht's] interpretation, one can easily follow his train of thought, because it is a sketch of those horizons from which Bach drew his compositional ideas and which directly relate to *The Art of Fugue*.[4]

Detlef Gojowy finds Eggebrecht's work to be a fundamentally new kind of Bach study— subjective, but, at the same time, surgically precise.

> He [Eggebrecht] illuminates Bach's posthumous work apart from all previous analytical arguments relative to the sequence of the individual fugues and canons that comprise the work, and discusses Bach's involvement with the meaning of the work's compositional substance. Eggebrecht is therefore exploring a region of musicological analysis, which for the most part, has been ignored in previous research on the origins of Bach's works. In all of this, Eggebrecht operates with caution and microscopic

---

[2] See chapter 1, p.9.

[3] Hermann Conen, review of *Bachs Kunst der Fuge: Erscheinung und Deutung* by Hans Heinrich Eggebrecht (München: R. Piper, 1984), *Concerto: Das Magazin für alte Musik* 2 (October-November 1985): 57.

[4] Wilfried Gruhn, review of *Bachs Kunst der Fuge: Erscheinung und Deutung* by Hans Heinrich Eggebrecht (München: R. Piper, 1984), *Musik und Bildung* 17 (May, 1985): 381.

precision, thereby applying the kind of interpretive standard to the works of Bach and Baroque music that were applied earlier only to the works of Scriabin or Webern.[5]

The kind of musicology found in this book is far different from many other historical and analytical studies on *The Art of Fugue;* that is, Eggebrecht stresses a workable interpretation of aesthetic content, musical rhetoric, and compositional intention rather than simply establishing historical and analytical facts. It is a curious serendipity that Joseph Kerman published his *Contemplating Music: Challenges to Musicology* at about the same time as the first German printing of Eggebrecht's *Bachs Kunst der Fuge.*[6] In *Contemplating Music,* Kerman calls for an approach to music scholarship that is oriented away from positivism and more towards criticism (criticism in the broad sense; i.e., "the study of the meaning and value of art works").[7]

Kerman argues that "there is something wrong with a discipline which spends (or spent) so much more of its time establishing texts than thinking about the texts thus established."[8] Later, he claims that Bach studies are particularly plagued by this difficulty.

> Bach research has for some time been poised on the brink of the classic positivistic dilemma: more and more facts, and less and less confidence in interpreting them.[9]

The reticence with which Eggebrecht approaches his preface and maintains to some degree throughout the entire book, seems to corroborate Kerman's view that "distrust of interpretation is programmatic among the traditional German Bach scholars."[10] This point was somewhat underscored when, in a letter to me, Eggebrecht seemed almost astonished that there was enough interest in this kind of interpretive study to produce a translation. Despite the fact that the author

---

[5] Detlef Gojowy, review of *Bachs Kunst der Fuge: Erscheinung und Deutung* by Hans Heinrich Eggebrecht (München: R. Piper, 1984), *Neue Zeitschrift für Musik* 146/3 (March 1985): 56.

[6] Eggebrecht's *Bachs Kunst der Fuge* was first published in December 1984 and Kerman's *Contemplating Music* appeared in 1985.

[7] Joseph Kerman, *Contemplating Music: Challenges to Musicology* (Cambridge, Mass.: Harvard University Press, 1985): 16.

[8] Kerman, *Contemplating Music,* p.48.

[9] Kerman, *Contemplating Music,* p.54.

[10] Kerman, *Contemplating Music,* p.54.

comes from the generation of German scholars that Kerman directly confronts, it is clear that Eggebrecht's interpretive approach lies close to those methodologies (based on criticism) which are advocated in *Contemplating Music*. One can only hope that Eggebrecht's *Bachs Kunst der Fuge*, with its careful reliance on musical analysis, historical research and musical intuition will prove to be a model for other such critical/interpretive studies of single works.

Returning to the question with which I began this foreword, just what does all this have to do with a composer-theorist turned translator? For more than twenty years, I have been teaching music courses to undergraduate music majors. Teaching "the facts" of theory and history or vocal and instrumental technique is something that is usually done reasonably well in college and university music departments. However, making good music is not just a matter of acquiring necessary technique and knowing facts. To be a truly successful performer, one must be able to turn analytical and historical facts and creative intuition about a piece of music into a relevant, critical, and individual point of view. A masterful technique is then the vehicle which the performer uses to communicate that point of view.

Though all young musicians learn about music by imitating and heeding the advice of their teachers, music study in a university often creates an environment where students simply, and often blindly, follow the directives of their instructors. Whether due to naivete, laziness, or fear of consequences, this problem is just as real in theory and musicology classes as it is in applied lessons. It has been my impression that most programs of music study (at least at the undergraduate level) do not often help the average music student begin to acquire the skills and confidence it takes to make individual interpretive decisions. As a result, I have heard hundreds of dull and unimaginative student performances, to say nothing of the papers I have had to read. In an attempt to provide an alternative path for music students, some of my colleagues and I have been involved in a team effort to design new courses that better help students integrate analytical skills, historical research and performance practices in such a way that they can both feel the excitement and see the musical results of building workable, individual (or consensus) interpretations of the pieces they are performing. We call these courses seminars in Analysis for Performance.

It is because of my interest in a music pedagogy which stresses a synthesis of the various (traditional) musical disciplines that I came to the final decision to translate Eggebrecht. What is so attractive about this book is that the author presents a scholarly but highly subjective point of view, which he then attempts to substantiate by introducing salient historical facts and analytical observations. Eggebrecht's brief and provocative text provides precisely the kind of integration of research, analysis, and intuitive processes that I would like to see my students begin to emulate. In short, it is a study that I can hold up as model of musicological inquiry.

Since I am a musician, this translation is primarily intended for use by English-reading music students and scholars, as well as by musicians who have performed or are contemplating a performance of *The Art of Fugue.* Nevertheless, it has been pointed out to me by several theologians that this book might also find a niche in the areas of history of theology or theology and the arts. Certain individuals working as church musicians or studying for the music ministry may also find this text and its approach both interesting and enlightening.

Although the German edition does not make use of footnotes, I have added them here to simplify translation of some of the author's parenthetical remarks and to help clarify certain points. My observations and comments will always appear in brackets; e.g., [Translator's note.] I have also added extra annotations to the author's musical examples to make some of the more important musical features easier to find at a glance. In addition, I slightly expanded four of the author's examples (Ex. 18, 25, 38a, and 50) in order to include some of the adjacent materials to which he refers in the text, and I took the liberty of adding one short additional example (Ex. 38b) so that I could more easily draw attention to cited materials.

Translating a treatise which makes many philosophical, theological, and rhetorical references was not always a straightforward task. For that reason, there may be some who will disagree with the way I handled a number of difficult-to-translate German terms and phrases.[11] Although there were some places where literal translation proved unworkable or impossible, to the best of my ability I have attempted to convey the sense and spirit of Eggebrecht's prose, while keeping the English as readable as possible.

I could not have undertaken a project like this without a great deal of moral and professional support. I am especially grateful to my wife, Jane, and my two daughters, Brittany and Allyson, who have provided me with encouragement and love during the past several years while I worked on not one, but two book-length translations. The year we spent together in Germany can only partially compensate them for their many sacrifices. I am also grateful to Iowa State University, which granted me a faculty improvement leave, in part so that I could finish the first draft of this translation. In addition, the College of Liberal Arts and Sciences at I.S.U. generously provided me with a grant to help defray the cost of final page preparation. I am indebted to my bright and tireless undergraduate research assistant, Joanne Wilson, who helped with both the final editing of the manuscript and the production of camera-ready materials for the publisher. I am also most grateful to my friend and colleague Dr. Alfred Kracher, and to my student Eric Petersen, who spent hours in the thankless job of proofreading the manuscript. Hearty thanks to the staff at Iowa State University Press who have

---

[11] The German terms *Sein* and *Dasein* were especially difficult to translate (see chapter 1, footnote 14).

been so warm and helpful in guiding this project to completion; especially former director Richard Kinney; chief editor Bill Silag; and production manager Robert Campbell. My deepest appreciation to Professor Herbert Schueller, who reviewed two drafts of the manuscript, and who offered countless valuable suggestions for improvement. I also wish to acknowledge my parents, Dr. Merle P. and Mrs. Elsie E. Prater, who provided me with a childhood home environment where love for learning and music could freely flow. They have supported me in countless ways, materially and spiritually, and I will always be grateful.

Finally, such a project would not have been possible had it not been for the motivation produced by my Analysis for Performance students. These hardy undergraduates, who despair of leaving any stones unturned, and who have enlightened peers and mentors alike with their lecture-recitals, have never failed to challenge me, inspire me, and hold me to my highest ideals. I dedicate this translation to them and to all musician/scholars who are not afraid to take a point of view and defend it.

JEFFREY L. PRATER

Ames, Iowa
June 1993

AUTHOR'S PREFACE

From the German Edition

I have wanted to write this book for a long time, but could never summon up the necessary courage. The initial ideas for my interpretation of J.S. Bach's *The Art of Fugue* came to me years ago during a time of intense study, and as these ideas have "hounded" me ever since, I have decided to record them here, in spite of the fact that they remain in rudimentary form and cannot be proved. Indeed, I introduce the goal and significance of this interpretation only by way of isolated arguments and I confirm my conclusions only circumstantially.

Perhaps it is advancing age that gives me the freedom to write about ideas which, from the start, cannot be proved, or perhaps my instinct tells me that an attempt to prove such an interpretation is really unnecessary anyway, since it does not depend upon exhaustive scholarly research. (I am confident, nonetheless, even in those places where my interpretation must be rejected on scholarly grounds, that the scholar will find my arguments and ideas to be interesting and worthwhile.) Perhaps the most important reason for producing this book, however, is the hope that the musical materials of *The Art of Fugue* will justify my interpretation, and, conversely, that my interpretation may provide some unique insights into the musical materials of the work.

There is hardly another musical work that contains so many unresolved problems as this late work of Bach. Even in the frequently encountered phrase, "The last Contrapunctus, the quadruple fugue in Bach's *The Art of Fugue* . . .," almost every word carries with it a question. Are we to assume that this incomplete fugue, written in Bach's own hand but without any inscription, was really intended to be a fugue constructed from four subjects, despite its designation in the first printed edition as a fugue constructed from three subjects? Does this fugue belong to *The Art of Fugue* at all, and if so, was it really planned to be the last fugue of the cycle?[1] Why is the "quadruple fugue" entitled *Contrapunctus*

---

[1] [Translator's note: This incomplete fugue is not found in the portion of the autograph materials generally called "The Berlin Autograph" (BWV 1080:1-14), but rather on five loose autograph pages in a folio labeled, in another hand, "Zum Original Manuscript der 'Kunst der Fuge' / von J.S. Bach / Fünf einzelne Blätter / in Querfolio" (BWV 1080:19).]

rather than *Fugue?* Finally, since the title *The Art of Fugue* is found in another hand in the autograph manuscript, can we actually be certain that it accurately conveys the composer's intentions?

For good reason, there have been many philosophical treatises written about *The Art of Fugue,* and although such writings are essential to the study of music, it is not my intention to set forth another such scholarly book here. I shall cite outside sources only as interpretation requires or when a particular reading might help clarify certain important questions raised by the musical materials. For the most part, however, I shall not depend upon outside resources, since it is my intention to provide analysis and to discuss debatable issues. Therefore, this book should not be considered a scholarly work, but rather the investigation of a personal and subjective theory. Nevertheless, the sources to which I am indebted, and which might be helpful to the reader, are organized under appropriate headings in the appended topical bibliography.

Bach's *The Art of Fugue* is held in great awe, and scarcely any other work in the history of music suggests so many artistic possibilities. At the same time, however, this cycle of fugues and canons has thoroughly mystified many of those who have attempted analysis. Without a doubt it was more practical for Bach to demonstrate his grasp of the interconnections between contrapuntal technique and aesthetic content in a musical composition than it would have been for him to have described these same relationships in a theoretical treatise, text-demonstration or essay. Practical origins of this work aside, however, I am convinced that Bach relied upon a specific extramusical idea to control the invention and development of the musical materials in *The Art of Fugue.* Therefore, my interpretation seeks to reveal an aesthetic meaning concealed within the work's musical substance. Since I am involving myself in unprovable matters, it is altogether possible that this book will only further add to the mystery which enshrouds the work; it is also possible, however, that my ideas may just be able to deal with that mystery on its own ground.

It should be quite evident from what I have said above that I consider this book as more of an essay than a monograph. I do not intend to treat all of the questions raised by the work or provide a complete analysis of its materials. Instead, this book should be regarded as a subjectively interpreted introduction to *The Art of Fugue.* This interpretation will act as a predetermined starting point for both selection and analysis of significant portions of the score, which, in turn, will be used as evidence that supports my interpretation. Though it would be best to study *The Art of Fugue* in its entirety, the scope of this book will allow me to cover only selected passages. Nevertheless, it is my hope that the following pages will succeed in stimulating further interest in the legitimacy of my interpretation.

J.S. Bach's *The Art of Fugue*

1

The B-A-C-H Theme

T he greater part of the first printed edition of *The Art of Fugue* was supervised by Johann Sebastian Bach himself, but after the composer's death, his son Carl Philipp Emanuel Bach (hereafter abbreviated C.P.E.) completed the task of preparing the work for publication. *The Art of Fugue* appeared in print sometime between autumn 1751 and Easter 1752. Although Bach did not live to complete the final movement, he was able to introduce three of its subjects and contrapuntally combine them. The third of these three subjects begins with the pitches B-A-C-H, but directly after it appears in counterpoint against both previously employed subjects, the texture breaks apart and the music suddenly ends.[1]

There are several questions that come to mind as we consider both the way this unfinished movement has been traditionally explained, and the role it plays in the entire work. There is little doubt that the movement actually belongs to *The Art of Fugue*. One of the many pieces of evidence supporting this conclusion is that all three of its subjects can be derived from the ground theme.[2] The reason why the final movement remained incomplete was answered by C.P.E. On the last page of his father's autograph manuscript[3] he wrote, "In this fugue, where

---

[1] [Translator's note: From this point on, it will be understood that the German spelling of the pitches B-A-C-H will refer to its English-language equivalent Bb-A-C-B♮.]

[2] These derivations will be discussed in detail later. [Translator's note: The term "ground theme" is used by the author to refer to the initial subject of *Contrapunctus I*, whose variations and metamorphoses provide subject (and other) material for all of the subsequent movements. For this reason, *The Art of Fugue* is often called monothematic. During the course of the book, Eggebrecht will explain how the ground theme functions as a generating source for many of the specific musical materials in the work.]

[3] [Translator's note: BWV 1080:19; see footnote 1 in Author's Preface.]

the name *BACH* appears in the countersubject, the composer died."[4] C.P.E. added further details in a short explanation placed at the front of the first printed copies of *The Art of Fugue.* Bach was, "because of his eye disease and approaching death, in no condition to shape adequately the third section of the final fugue and bring it to a conclusion."

Despite the eye trouble which had long plagued him, it is likely that the composer was at work on *The Art of Fugue* until the time of his eye surgery at the end of March 1750. Bach's obituary *(Nekrolog)* reports that "[t]he operation went very badly. In addition to losing the use of his eyesight, his entire constitution, otherwise thoroughly healthy, was completely upset by the effects of the operation and by the application of harmful treatments and medications. . . ." Furthermore, a second eye operation at the beginning of April produced the same unfortunate results, so that Bach could no longer compose. From this point, he was "nearly always ill" until his death on July 28.

It is all but certain that the unfinished fugue was not intended to begin a new group of fugues, even though *The Art of Fugue,* as a whole, proceeds from one group of related fugal types to another.[5] Instead, it is probably best to consider this complex though fragmentary movement as a single large fugue whose function is to provide an ending for the entire work. For this reason, we shall refer to it as the *closing fugue* of the work.

It is also quite certain that this movement was planned to be a quadruple fugue instead of a triple fugue. As we will discuss later, it is likely that Bach intended to reintroduce the ground theme as the fourth subject of the closing fugue, and then set it in counterpoint against the three other subjects. Assuming this theory is correct, an analogy can be drawn between the group of four [simple] fugues which appear at the beginning of the entire work and the complex four-subject fugue which was planned for its conclusion (Ex. 1).[6]

The three extant subjects of the closing fugue are contrapuntally combined just seven measures before the fugue abruptly breaks off (see the four braced lower staves in Ex. 1). The bass voice takes the seven pitches of the first subject; the alto takes the second subject with its characteristic stream of eighth notes; the tenor takes the third subject with its B-A-C-H opening pitches, while the soprano maintains a contrapuntally free voice which imitates elements of the second

---

[4] Here, the term *countersubject* should be interpreted to mean theme-against-theme [rather than as a technical term denoting a regular contrapuntal accompaniment to a fugue subject. That is, the author considers the melodic material in the fragment beginning with the pitches B-A-C-H to be a true theme [third subject] which appears in counterpoint against the first subject (see measures 234-39, bass; 235-39, tenor)].

[5] Four simple fugues are followed by three counterfugues, . . . etc. See Table 2, p.114.

[6] It is also possible to conclude that this quadruple fugue is a single fugue containing four separate fugues.

EXAMPLE 1

Closing Fugue Fragment: last seven measures with added Ground Theme Line

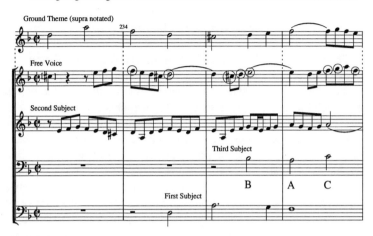

subject. The entry of all three subjects in this passage also permits us [hypotheti-cally] to add the ground theme to the contrapuntal texture (see the supranotated line in Ex. 1). In fact, if we take a closer look at the soprano's "free" voice, we can see that it already outlines the pitches of the ground theme (circled notes).

Up to the present, nearly all scholars agree that the "BACH theme" is the last of the many subjects in *The Art of Fugue* to be derived from the ground theme. Furthermore, there is unanimous agreement that Bach intentionally spelled his own surname in the first four pitches of the third subject. Why this spelling of the name "Bach" occurs here is the only real question. Before directly considering this question, however, we shall briefly discuss the concept of note-name symbolism in order to familiarize ourselves with an aspect of Bach's compositional process that may prove helpful later when we consider other types of symbolism in *The Art of Fugue.*

Note-name Symbolism

The first four tones at the beginning of the third subject derive their meaning from an extramusical source. That is, our recognition of the name "Bach" in these pitches does not proceed directly from the tones as they are heard; rather, the word "Bach" is intentionally transferred to the four sounding tones from the letters of the alphabet which spell the composer's name. It is possible to associate the composer's name with these four tones only because the notes are labeled with the letters B-A-C-H; the sounding pitches themselves do not directly represent the name at all. It is only because of the way the musical tones are alphabetically labeled in the German language that any connection between sounding pitches and "Bach" is possible.[7] These four tones cannot convey to the ear as specific a meaning as their respective letter-name symbols, because the aesthetic content of these tones is not sufficient to communicate such an idea. In order for this symbolism to be effective, an alphabetically labeled system of musical notation is required. In the case of these particular tones, it is absolutely essential to know that they are defined by the letter-names B-A-C-H before any intended meaning can be recognized and understood.

Though it is possible to ascribe a meaning to any tone or group of tones, it is necessary for the composer to transfer that meaning into the aesthetic domain from a clearly defined extramusical source; that is, if the listener is to recognize and comprehend the symbol. The presence of these obvious and easily interpreted note-names in the third subject of the closing fugue suggest that Bach embraced this kind of symbolism and did not consider it at all foreign to his compositional process.

The Double Discant Clausula

Until now, it has been generally accepted that the B-A-C-H motto was simply the composer's way of musically autographing *The Art of Fugue.*[8] Although this assumption cannot be proved, it is certainly a plausible theory. I should like to introduce another possibility, however, based on the presupposition that *The Art of Fugue* unfolds from a central metaphysical idea. In order to

---

[7] It is important to remember that specific note-name symbols are not universally employed in all notational systems [even across Western cultures]. In France, for example, the pitches b-a-c-h would be represented by the note-names: *si be-mol—la—ut—si,* which do not carry the same extramusical symbolic meaning.

pursue this interpretation, however, we must study the entire third subject of the closing fugue, not just its first four pitches (B-A-C-H).[9]

It is quite possible that Bach did not so much engrave his name in the closing fugue to denote authorship, but rather to say: "I desire to reach, and am in the process of reaching, toward the *Tonic*—I am identified with it." An examination of the musical materials indeed confirms that the tonic note (d) is the central reference pitch of every movement. In fact, d is both the starting pitch and goal pitch of the overall musical structure in the work as a whole. Therefore, the addition of a *double discant clausula* to the pitches B-A-C-H in the third subject of the closing fugue is very significant.[10]

To understand how this remarkable cadence formula supports my interpretation of *The Art of Fugue,* it is necessary to consider the role that repetition played in musical compositions written during the time of Bach.

According to the Baroque-era doctrine of musical-rhetorical figures, every repetition of a melodic or harmonic element becomes an important point of emphasis; such repetition is clearly present in the double discant clausula at the close of the third subject (Ex. 2). Furthermore, the double discant clausula also exhibits the characteristics of a rhetorical device called *polysyndeton.*[11] A

EXAMPLE 2

Closing Fugue: Third Subject

---

[8] This practice could be considered similar to the name engraving done in building stones by master builders and stonemasons during the Middle Ages. In fact, Bach's name is actually engraved twice in *The Art of Fugue*— once on the title page, where the composer's name is printed, and here in the first four notes of the work's last extant subject.

[9] Instead of simply calling this subject the "B-A-C-H theme" (as is traditional), we will refer to it, in this text, by its complete name, the "B-A-C-H-C♯-D-C♯-D theme" [or by its abbreviation, the "B-A-C-H-C♯-D theme"]. [Translator's note: Though there is an extra sixteenth note h (b♮) interpolated between the second c♯-d pair in the third subject of the closing fugue, it should be considered only an unstructural ornamentation here.]

[10] A *discant clausula* is a melodic cadence formula in early music, where the leading tone of the scale demands immediate resolution to the tonic. A *double discant clausula* is the immediate repetition of a discant clausula [i.e., c♯-d, c♯-d in the key of d minor].

[11] *Polysyndeton* literally means a succession of conjunct similar articulations.

melodic motive that is emphasized or intensified by modified repetition shows the influence of polysyndeton.

The double discant clausula at the end of the third subject contains a clear example of polysyndeton, since the second clausula is more highly ornamented than the first. Bach also gradually increases the durational emphasis of the structural pitches within the complete cadence figure. The tied-over tonic pitch (d) [measures 195-96] is much longer in duration than the eighth-note leading tone (c♯) which precedes it. The next leading tone [measure 196] is now metrically stressed and lengthened to a half note. Though the final tonic [measure 197] only appears as a half note, it is possible to increase its durational influence if we take the trill regulation from Bach's autograph manuscript into account.[12]

Because Bach connected the pitches B-A-C-H to this emphatic cadential process, I cannot believe that he only intended to say, "I composed this." Rather, appending the double discant clausula to the B-A-C-H motto seems to say, "I am identified with the *Tonic* and it is my desire to reach it." Interpreted more broadly, this statement could read: "Like you, I am human; I am in need of salvation; I am certain in the hope of that salvation, and I have been saved by grace." Indeed, there is an unmistakable similarity between the conviction established in this interpretation and the hymn text of Bach's last chorale setting:[13]

> *"Vor deinen Thron tret ich hiermit . . .*
> *Nimm meine Seel in deine Händ . . .*
> *Gott Sohn, du hast mich durch dein Blut*
> *erlöset von der Höllenglut."*

> (Before Thy throne here I stand . . .
> Take my soul in your hands . . .
> Son of God, you have saved me
> by your blood from the fires of Hell.)

---

[12] [Translator's note: Although there may be several workable realizations for this trill figure, the tonic note (d) will certainly be alternated with the leading tone (c♯). The rapid alternation of these two pitches forms a mixture of tonic and leading tone, which not only heightens the resolution-seeking tension of the leading tone, but also produces a strong anticipation of the tonic. The author implies that the presence of the pitch d in this trill has the effect of extending the influence of the final tonic pitch backward from measure 197 into the second half of measure 196. It should be noted that this trill figure is found only in the autograph manuscript and does not appear in the first printed edition or in most subsequent publications of *The Art of Fugue* .]

[13] The so-called "deathbed chorale." Its relationship to *The Art of Fugue* will be discussed at length in chapter 4.

I freely admit that this interpretation can never be proved. In fact, such an interpretation hardly dares venture out into today's world. Ideas like this are viewed with great suspicion and are often immediately discounted on the grounds that they present an ideologically corrupted analysis of Bach's intentions. I have made allowance for just such a reaction, however. So far, I have only presented my case; in the remaining pages, I shall present evidence in an attempt to convince the jury.

Chromaticism in the B-A-C-H-C♯-D Theme

If we are to come to a conclusion about the validity of my interpretation, we must now continue our discussion of the third subject of the closing fugue and then examine a number of musical materials from other parts of the work.

First, as may have already been anticipated, it is necessary to make a distinction between diatonic and chromatic pitch materials in *The Art of Fugue*. My first premise is that the diatonic materials of this work relate to the perfect and complete nature of God *(Sein),* and that chromatic materials relate to the sinful and troubled condition of the human soul *(Dasein).*[14]

The "B-A-C-H-C♯-D theme" belongs to the chromatic side. In fact, if the pitches of this subject are arranged in ascending or descending order, a chromatic scale within the interval of a perfect fourth is produced (Ex. 3).

In musical composition during the Baroque, a chromatic scale within the interval of a perfect fourth was called *passus duriusculus.*[15] The use of passus

EXAMPLE 3

Closing Fugue: B-A-C-H-C♯-D Theme

complete chromatic within a perfect fourth
(passus duriusculus)

---

[14] [Translator's note: The terms *Sein* and *Dasein* are difficult to translate directly. Although *Sein* is literally "a state of being," the manner in which the author uses this term also includes a sense of the eternal or everlasting, roughly equivalent to the English expression "The Alpha and Omega" or the Biblical reference to God as "The [eternal] I Am." *Dasein* is literally "a state of existence," but is differentiated from *Sein* in that it implies a "created existence." Starting from this implication of "created existence" the author employs *Dasein* when he refers to the fallen and incomplete spiritual condition (in the Christian understanding) of humanity apart from union with God.]

[15] *Passus duriusculus* literally means "a somewhat difficult passage."

duriusculus was considered an unnatural procedure, and students were warned
to "watch out" before attempting its use, since it creates *cross-relations* when a
single voice is set in counterpoint against itself.[16]

Because the employment of passus duriusculus is a departure from the more
usual diatonic order of pitches, it became associated, in Baroque musical
rhetoric, with a category of words including *sin, guilt, misery, distress,* and
death. There are innumerable spots in the vocal music of Bach where such words
are associated with passus duriusculus.   Some important examples are the
ostinato bass in the first chorus of the Cantata No.12, *"Weinen, Klagen, Sorgen,
Zagen, Angst und Not sind der Christen Tränenbrot"* (Weeping, Grieving,
Sorrow, Timidity, Fear and Affliction are the Christian's Bread of Tears);[17] the
chromatic passages accompanying the words: *"Ächzen und erbärmlich Weinen"*
(moaning and merciful weeping) from Cantata No.13; *"Wer Sünde tut"* (who-
soever sins) from Cantata No.54; *"Mein großer Jammer bleibt danieden"* (my
great wretchedness remains here below) from Cantata No. 60; and *"Sein
menschlich Wesen machet euch den Engels-Herrlichkeiten gleich"* (God's
human substance makes you equal with the angels) from Cantata No. 91.
Generally, Bach employs chromatic materials when a text speaks of God, in the
person of Christ, taking upon Himself the sinful nature of humanity.

Because of the highly chromatic nature of its materials, the B-A-C-H-C#-D
theme could be interpreted as a musical representation of the composer's human
condition *(Dasein)*; a condition which Bach understood to be sinful and in need
of salvation.[18] Since the pitch materials of this subject are not presented in scale
order, however, the chromatic connections between the pitches are somewhat
obscured. In fact, the actual order of these six pitches gives the subject a unique
character. Even though all of the pitches in the subject are chromatically
contained within a perfect fourth, the chromatic relationship between the pitches
is relatively weak because the pitches B-A-C-H are emphatically connected with
the tonic (d) through the double discant clausula. This somewhat scrambled set
of chromatic tones actually forms a melodic pattern much more characteristic of
diatonic space. Because the pitches b♭-a-c are scale-tone members of the d
natural-minor scale, and as it is necessary to avoid the difficult-to-sing augmented second (b♭-c#) when approaching the leading tone (c#) from below, the
theme turns at its fourth note to b♮, a member of the ascending melodic-minor
scale (Ex. 4).

---

[16] *Cross-relations* are created when a chromatic half step (e.g., e♮-e♭, f#-f♮, etc.) occurs in immediate
or close succession between different voices of a musical composition.

[17] Bach also later used this same bass-line ostinato in the *Crucifixus* of the B-minor Mass.

[18] [Translator's note: Throughout this book, the author interprets the B-A-C-H motto and the
chromatic materials associated with it to be a figurative representation the composer's own
humanness. In the author's words, the B-A-C-H motto is the musical "I" of the work.]

EXAMPLE 4

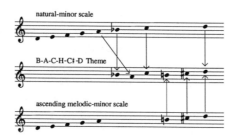

The pitch relationships in the B-A-C-H-C♯-D theme are both derived from and refer back to the ground theme (Ex. 5). The half-step returning-tone figures d-c♯-d and a-b♭-a mark the respective mid-points of both the ground theme and its inversion. Thus, the normal and inverted forms of the ground theme already contain the two most important musical gestures that shape the third subject of the closing fugue—the downward-resolving (Phrygian) half step (b♭-a), and the upward-resolving, leading-tone half step (c♯-d).

EXAMPLE 5

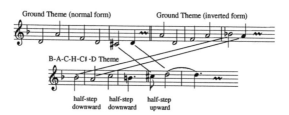

As opposed to the release of tension produced by the leading-tone half step (c♯-d), the returning-tone motive a-b♭-a, derived from the center of the inverted ground theme, manifests a *pathopoetic* character.[19] Even though this latter motive is diatonic to d minor, it appears prominently as both the melodic climax and central axis of the inverted ground theme. In my interpretation, the human conditions of sin and sorrow will be musically represented by this returning-tone motive. There are actually two remnants of this motive still preserved in the B-A-C-H-C♯-D theme—the half-step motive b♭-a and its forward-thrusting sequential repetition c-b♮.

---

[19] The rhetorical term *pathopoeia* literally means "solemn or sorrowful."

Gradatio is the Baroque musical-rhetorical term used to describe a sequential melodic repetition at a higher pitch level.[20] The subject's opening pair of two-note motives (bb-a/c-b♮) is an obvious example of gradatio, but this device is employed in a less conspicuous way as well. The double discant clausula (c#-d/c#-d) produces a type of gradatio with the downward-sequenced half steps (bb-a/c-b♮) from the B-A-C-H motto. The two upward-resolving leading tone-to-tonic figures are actually an emphatically repeated inversion (at a higher pitch level) of the opening two downward-resolving half-step figures.

To summarize, the discant clausula in the B-A-C-H-C#-D theme functions in three ways: 1) It connects the note-name symbolism of B-A-C-H to the tonic; 2) it helps produce diatonic implications in the subject, despite the presence of three conjunct half-step motives contained within a perfect fourth; and 3) the emphatic repetition of the ending c#-d figures finds additional motivation (gradatio, pathopoeia) in the pitch sequence bb-a/c-b♮ at the beginning of the subject.

All three of these technical and semantically interrelated musical devices function to connect *Bach* with the *Tonic*. The desire for unity with the tonic is confirmed by the very presence of these emphatic gestures, while the fulfillment of this unity is represented by a final and conclusive resolution to the tonic pitch. We must remember, however, that these musical gestures, like all of the materials of the B-A-C-H-C#-D theme, are actually derived from the middle of the ground theme and its inversion.

---

[20] *Gradatio* literally means "climax."

2

Aesthetic and Symbolic Meaning in the First Two Subjects of the Closing Fugue

The First Subject of the Closing Fugue

B ecause of its simple structure, the initial subject of the closing fugue seems, at first glance, to have so little in common with the ground theme that it appears to be independently conceived. Although it is the most elementary subject employed in *The Art of Fugue,* its melodic structure can be derived from the opening notes of the ground theme.

The initial three pitches of the ground theme and the first four pitches of the first closing-fugue subject are indeed quite similar. As is shown in Example 6, the pitch materials of these two themes correspond even more closely, if we consider the fifth and sixth notes (g,a) of the closing-fugue subject to be added tones inserted between the third and fourth notes of the ground theme (f,d).[1] However, these two whole notes are important structural pitches in the first closing-fugue subject, since they are needed to form the subject's mirror-image pitch symmetry.[2] Both the ground theme and the first subject of the closing fugue also share the same basic melodic contour.[3]

The first four pitches of the ground theme and the entire first subject of the closing fugue strongly outline the most fundamental sonority in the key of d-minor: the tonic triad (d-f-a). By limiting the pitch materials to just four tones

---

[1] [Translator's note: Since the quarter note (g) in the first subject of the closing fugue is comparatively shorter than the surrounding notes, and since it occurs in a metrically unstressed position, the author implies (but does not directly state) that it functions more as a passing tone than as a structural pitch.]

[2] The pitches of the subject are exactly the same from the beginning to the middle as they are from the end to the middle.

[3] The midpoint pitches of the two subjects are both approached and departed by ascending and descending melodic motion. Nevertheless, it should be noted that the two midpoint pitches themselves are different. The midpoint of the ground theme is the leading tone (c♯), whereas the third of the tonic triad (f) is the midpoint of the first closing-fugue subject.

(d-f-g-a) and by allowing its melodic motion to progress only by perfect fifths or major seconds, Bach further reinforces the tonal stability of the first closing-fugue subject. It should also be observed that neither the eighth-note figure (introduced in the ground theme by the syncopated, tied-over half note) nor the half-step motives (e-f and d-c♯-d) occur in the first subject of the closing fugue.[4] Therefore, this subject does not contain the same forward rhythmic thrust or pathopoetic character as the ground theme.

EXAMPLE 6

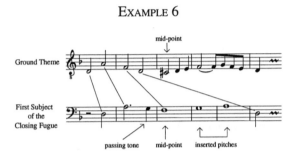

The first subject of the closing fugue, with its lack of half-step motion, contains the purest form of diatonic expression in *The Art of Fugue*. As a musical embodiment of stability and internal repose, I shall interpret this subject to be representative of the peaceful nature of God *(Sein)*. The strong and stable role this subject plays in the closing fugue is established, at the very beginning of the fugue, by its entry in the bass.[5]

The pure diatonic foundation of the first subject is particularly important when we consider its contrapuntal relationship to the B-A-C-H-C♯-D theme (third subject). Though the latter can also be derived from the ground theme, its highly chromatic materials stand in basic opposition to the purely diatonic elements found in the first subject. Nevertheless, the strong entry of the first subject [measure 234, bass] supplies a firm tonal footing for the subsequent entry of the B-A-C-H-C♯-D theme [measure 235, tenor]. The tonally stable first subject, which appears here in the bass, further aids the process by which the highly chromatic elements of the B-A-C-H-C♯-D theme are brought under the

---

[4] As will be discussed later, syncopation and running eighth-note figures are prominent elements in the second closing-fugue subject.

[5] The first closing-fugue subject is employed as though it were a *cantus firmus*. [Translator's note: "A *cantus firmus* is an existing melody that becomes the basis of a polyphonic composition through the addition of contrapuntal voices. . . . [It usually appears] in long notes that contrast with the more florid design of the other parts."—Willi Apel, ed., *Harvard Dictionary of Music,* second ed. (Cambridge, Mass.: Belknap Press, 1969): 130-32.]

diatonic control of d-minor.[6]   Although the chromatic materials of the B-A-C-H-C#-D theme provide counterthematic contrast to the pure diatonicism of the first subject, these chromatic materials are contrapuntally bound to the tonal stability of the first subject and are aesthetically connected to the first subject's character of "internal repose."[7]

Musical Numerology

The first subject of the closing fugue contains a total of seven pitches. Since it is possible that Bach intended this group of seven pitches to be a number symbol, it is necessary to briefly discuss musical numerology.

We must disregard many books and articles dealing with number symbols in the works of Bach. In fact, countless highly speculative writings have brought the study of "Bach the numerologist" into thorough disrepute. Therefore, when approaching Bach's use of number symbols, one must work with the utmost care and discretion. From the beginning, especially considering a textless work like *The Art of Fugue,* it is difficult, if not impossible, to conclusively prove the presence of a number symbol. Furthermore, if a musical passage suggests the presence of a number symbol, it is important that we attempt to determine just how valid our conclusions about the meaning of that symbol are. For that reason, it is safest to limit our inquiry to those few integers which, as a group, were known to possess symbolic significance during the Baroque.

It is particularly important to make certain that the specific meaning of a number symbol does not contradict the basic aesthetic character of an associated musical passage. If this principle is followed, our study of number symbols is not so likely to lead us into blatantly esoteric or allegorical conclusions about the music. Rather, it becomes possible for both the specific and objective number symbol and the more subjective aesthetic content to mutually illumine and clarify one another. With this requirement firmly in place, the interpretation of a number symbol loses some of its autonomy. It should be noted, however, that any connection between a number symbol and the musical aesthetic can work in both directions; that is, it is also possible for the prevailing aesthetic character of a passage to point out, enlarge upon, and underscore the meaning of a number symbol.[8]

---

[6] The diatonic reinterpretation of chromatic elements in the B-A-C-H-C#-D theme was discussed in chapter 1.

[7] [Translator's note: Although the author used the term *countersubject* here in the German edition, it should be understood, once again, to mean *countertheme* (theme-against-theme). See chapter 1, footnote 4.]

[8] It must be remembered, however, that the number symbol itself serves only as evidence of association with an extramusical concept—it is not itself a proof of that association.

If a composer assigns a specific meaning to a particular number and if that number is identifiable in clearly set-off musical materials, then the presence of that number symbol will take on a significance that goes beyond its simple numerical value.[9] In such a case, the number and the musical materials associated with it can point toward or represent some extra-musical object or concept.[10]

As discussed in chapter 1, the spelling of the name "Bach" in the third subject of the closing fugue provides evidence that extramusical symbolism was an important aspect of the composer's creative process.[11] Indeed, the presence of the pitches B-A-C-H in the closing fugue argues vigorously that Bach freely linked extramusical symbols with his choice of musical materials. However, the intended meaning of such an association is only apparent if we have some foreknowledge of the extramusical symbol. Since a relatively simple symbolic relationship exists between a set of pitches and the notational letter names associated with those pitches, there is no question at all about the interpretation of the note-name symbols in the B-A-C-H motto.

We need to be more cautious when interpreting the meaning of a pure-number symbol, however. This is because a specific symbolic reference applied to a number is not as easy to determine as the meaning of a note-name symbol like B-A-C-H. To start with, it is impossible to ascertain whether or not a countable group of musical events is actually intended to be a number symbol. Furthermore, single numbers may symbolize many different objects or concepts, and specific symbolic references to a number can change in the course of time and be viewed differently from one tradition to another.

Since ancient times, the number seven has played an important role as the "perfect" or "holy" number for many nations and cultures.[12] The objects and ideas known to be symbolized by the number seven are so numerous that they are impossible to count. This is true even if we limit our discussion to the symbolic use of "seven" in Christian theology during the late Baroque. It only takes a glance at one section of a text by the Protestant organist, Andreas Werckmeister

---

[9] For example, the number of pitches in a theme, the number of thematic entries, the number of measures or number of voices in a section of a work, a number in the meter signature, the number of a movement in a work, etc.

[10] The discussion here pertains only to pure-number symbolism and <u>not</u> to alpha-numeric symbolism. Alpha-numeric symbolism, where numbers become substituted for letters of the alphabet, will be discussed later in this chapter.

[11] See pp.5-6.

[12] For example, the seven days of creation, the seven planets [known to the ancient world], the seven wonders of the world, the seven steps to the temple, seven-armed candlesticks, the seven [diatonic] pitches within the octave, etc.

[1645-1706], to confirm this.[13] Werckmeister wrote that the number seven is the "number of rest" (because God rested on the seventh day). It is also called the "number of the virgin." In addition, the number seven is also considered to be a *"holy number,* because only the Spirit of God can fathom its meaning." Furthermore, "God is known as a *Sevenfold Spirit."* Werckmeister also points out that the proportions for all musical consonances are derived from seven numbers (1-6 and 8). Seven, the "number of rest," does not itself take part in this derivation, however.[14] Werckmeister is by no means the only contemporary witness to the importance of numerological symbolism in the German late-Baroque. In fact, there were so many secret meanings attached to numbers that it is impossible, in specific cases, to come to accurate conclusions about the true meaning of a number symbol.

We shall now closely examine the first subject of the closing fugue and discuss: 1) its symmetry; 2) its pure diatonic construction and derivation from the d-minor triad;[15] and 3) my aesthetic interpretation of the subject as a representation of the peaceful nature of God *(Sein).*

---

[13] See the chapter entitled *Von der Zahlen geheimen Deutung* [on numbers with secret meanings] in: Andreas Werckmeister, *Musicalische Paradoxal-Discourse* (Quedlinburg, 1707).

[14] [Translator's note: In Pythagorean tuning, the ratio of frequencies of the lower tone of an octave to its upper note is 1:2; the perfect fifth, 2:3; the perfect fourth, 3:4; the major third, 4:5; the minor third, 5:6, the major sixth, 3:5; and the minor sixth 5:8. All these consonances can be derived from the first eight partials (excluding seven) of the natural harmonic series (see chart below). The seconds, sevenths and the tritone (dissonances) can not be derived from the first eight partials of the natural harmonic series.

Since the seventh partial is noticeably out-of-tune (flat) and, therefore, musically unusable, its presence in the natural harmonic series has created no small difficulty for musicians, theorists and instrument makers throughout the history of western music. Even theorists as recent as Hindemith have relied heavily on metaphysical explanations of the seventh partial. See: Paul Hindemith, *The Craft of Musical Composition,* trans. Arthur Mendel (New York: Schott, 1942; rev. 1945),1:38]

The Natural Harmonic Series
partials 1-8 (above D2*)

the seventh partial
is noticeably flat

* The octave classification system employed in this translation is the one suggested by the International Acoustical Society, where the C at approximately 16 Hz. is CØ, and where "middle-C is C4.

[15] As was previously discussed, the purely diatonic construction of this subject is further emphasized by its complete lack of half-steps.

It is possible that Bach intended to symbolize the "holy" number by limiting the first subject of the closing fugue to only seven notes. Moreover, this subject can be organized into two groups of pitches, one consisting of four tones and the other of three tones (d-a-g-f | g-a-d). This organizational scheme reflects the frequently encountered numerological premise that seven is the sum of the symbolic numbers four and three.[16]

As we have already discussed, the rhetorical goal of the seven-pitch first subject is to provide a strong diatonic foundation for the unification of B-A-C-H with the tonic.[17]   Furthermore, both the B-A-C-H-C♯-D theme (constructed to function in counterpoint with the ground theme) and the ground theme itself also fulfill the conditions that we have established for a connection between the musical aesthetic and an extramusical symbol.[18]

We cannot go much farther with our discussion of number symbolism in the first subject of the closing fugue, although we could incorporate into our discussion some observations about the perfectly symmetrical mirror-image pitch structure of the subject (d-a-g |f| g-a-d), or, perhaps, discuss the alternative possibility of a 2 + 3 + 2 pitch grouping (d-a |g-f-g| a-d). In fact, the latter closely approximates Augustine's theory on how the number seven came to be considered a perfect number. According to Augustine,[19] the number seven is the sum of the first even and divisible number (four),[20] and the first prime number (three). We might also apply a study of clever games *(Lusus ingenii)* to the first subject of the closing fugue, but while such a study might prove entertaining, nothing of great consequence would be learned from it. Dwelling on such conjectures would serve only to enlarge the already mountainlike stack of speculative literature on *The Art of Fugue,* and does nothing to help us establish an interpretive position worthy of debate.

---

[16] Broadly speaking, the number four symbolizes matters of the world and humankind *(Dasein),* whereas the number three symbolizes the Trinitarian Godhead *(Sein).*

[17] The unification of B-A-C-H with the tonic symbolizes the unification of human nature with the nature of God *(des Daseins mit dem Sein).*

[18] As was discussed in chapter 1, extramusical symbolism in the B-A-C-H-C♯-D theme is provided by both note-naming (B-A-C-H), and the rhetorical figures of *polysyndeton* (p.7) and *gradatio* (p.12) which are both contained in the double discant clausula. Also, the ground theme contains a possible reference to numeric symbolism, as it contains seven different pitches within its twelve note length.

[19] [Translator's note: St. Augustine, *The City of God,* Book 11, Section 31. Augustine's view is represented here by breaking the divisible number four into two groups of two pitches and placing them on both sides of a third group which contains three pitches (d-a |g-f-g| a-d).]

[20] [Translator's note: That is, the first even integer divisible by a number other than itself or one.]

Accompanimental Voices

The contrapuntal voices which accompany the subjects in *The Art of Fugue* also provide evidence for our interpretation. Of particular importance are those countervoices which appear regularly against a subject or subjects. Regularly recurring accompaniments to a fugue subject are known as *countersubjects.*[21]

Although not a true countersubject, one countervoice in the closing fugue [measures 16-21, tenor] exhibits a particularly strong chromatic opposition to the pure diatonic of the first subject (Ex. 7). Not only does this countervoice contain the complete scale-ordered chromatic within a perfect fourth, but it also presents all of the pitches of the B-A-C-H-C♯-D theme. In fact, this contrapuntal line contains the most purely chromatic ordering of the B-A-C-H-C♯-D theme in *The Art of Fugue.*

EXAMPLE 7

Closing Fugue

Bach is always careful to foreshadow and musically prepare both the thematic [subject] variations and the contrapuntal techniques he will employ at some later point in the work. The plan of *The Art of Fugue* also seems to demand that all the emerging thematic materials and contrapuntal techniques be able to trace their origins back to the ground theme.

In the countervoice shown in Example 7, we can observe a foreshadowing of the B-A-C-H-C♯-D theme in the pitches of the scale-ordered chromatic segment. In addition, this chromatic segment can be considered a foreshadowing of the connection that will take place between the pitches B-A-C-H-C♯-D and the first subject, when they are set in counterpoint against each other in the third section of the closing fugue. It is as if these same, though reordered, chromatic pitches are even here seeking unity with the first subject.[22]

The prominent pitch motive c♯-d is also frequently encountered in the first section of the closing fugue. This half-step motive is especially pronounced in the first post-expositional section, where the discant clausula figure (which later

---

[21] [Translator's note: Here the term *countersubject* returns to its usual meaning in the technical jargon of fugue. See chapter 1, footnote 4 .]

[22] [Translator's note: The first subject represents "the ground of being" (Sein und Besagen).]

connects B-A-C-H to diatonic space) appears repeatedly in the soprano countervoice against the inverted form of the first subject (Ex. 8).[23] The pitch sequence b-a and c-h also seems to be highlighted here.

EXAMPLE 8

Closing Fugue

The Second Subject of the Closing Fugue

Like the first subject, the second subject of the closing fugue (Ex. 9) is diatonic. Nevertheless, the character of the second subject stands in strong opposition to the first. Instead of "restful" rhythmic motion in half and whole notes, "running" eighth notes completely dominate the texture. Furthermore, the second subject does not share the first subject's pitch symmetry, but is asymmetrically constructed so that it seems to push inexorably forward. A prominent pathopoetic half-step figure (a-bb-a) is also associated with the melodic climax near the end of the second subject.

EXAMPLE 9

Closing Fugue

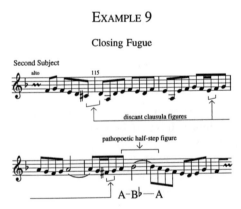

[23] [Translator's note: Bach introduces the inverted form of the first subject directly after the initial exposition of the closing fugue (measure 21, bass). In addition, the entire post-expositional section (measures 21-48) contains consecutively contrasting entries of both subject and inverted subject, as well as overlapping entrances *(stretto)* between normal and inverted forms of the subject.]

The characteristic rhythm and the artful melodic twisting at the beginning of the second subject can be traced back to materials found at the end of the ground theme (Ex. 10). In fact, the eighth-note motive that closes the ground theme is actually the generator of all forward-driving rhythmic motion in the entire work. The structure of the second subject of the closing fugue is yet another example of the importance of the ground theme as the primary source of musical materials in *The Art of Fugue*.

EXAMPLE 10

Bach's choice of specific materials is always motivated by the larger musical considerations of a composition; that is, Bach took pains to see that every detail of his score was significant and in the correct order vis-à-vis all other materials. This kind of careful compositional control certainly applies to the highly distinctive subjects of the closing fugue. Not only are all of these subjects designed to work in counterpoint against each other (in both normal and inverted forms), but each subject also maintains its own individual character. We can assume, therefore, that the closing-fugue subjects were probably invented to deliberately contrast with each other, since it is primarily through their individual characters that each of them remains distinct from the others.[24]

Certainly, the second subject, with its "running" eighth notes, fulfills both the conditions discussed above. It combines contrapuntally with the other closing-fugue subjects, while maintaining its own individual character. Moreover, the rhythmic construction of the second subject guarantees that there will be a constant eighth-note flow later when all the subjects are combined with each other. The "running" eighth notes of this theme also relieve the basic quarter-note pulse that rhythmically dominated the first section of the closing fugue.

This "running-note" second subject is characterized by forward rhythmic drive. It is resolute, restless and creative; in short, it is "alive." In addition to the pathopoetic half-step figure (a-bb-a) associated with the B-A-C-H-C♯-D theme, the second subject also contains the discant clausula (c♯-d) [Ex. 9, measures 115-116].[25] The significance of the "running theme" is that it mediates between the

---

[24] This is especially true since the subjects of the closing fugue are simultaneously employed in the second and third sections of this extended movement.

[25] Note also the two sixteenth-note discant clausuli (e-f and f♯-g), which are contained in the second subject (See Ex. 9, measures 116 and 118).

character of "peace" (which occurs in the first section of the fugue), and the symbolic unification of "human nature" with the "nature of God" (which occurs in the third section). Though the second subject certainly does not share the "peaceful" qualities of the first subject, it does appear as a countertheme to the first subject; and though the second subject does not itself symbolize the unification of the "human soul" with "God," it does combine contrapuntally with the B-A-C-H-C♯-D theme, and it seems to strive toward that unification.

Alpha-numeric Symbolism

The second subject contains forty-one pitches. This group of pitches could also have symbolic meaning, if we consider the possibility of *alphabetic-numeric* (from this point, *alpha-numeric*) symbolism. With alpha-numeric symbolism, every letter of the alphabet can be represented by a corresponding number (A = 1, B = 2, C = 3, etc.).[26] By this method, the surname "Bach" is represented by the number fourteen. That is, "Bach" can be numerically represented by the sum of the numbers which represent the letters B, A, C, and H $(2 + 1 + 3 + 8 = 14)$. Correspondingly, the name "J.S. Bach" can be represented by the number forty-one $(9 + 18 + 14 = 41)$, and the full name, "Johann Sebastian Bach," by the number one hundred fifty-eight.

The mind certainly does not [consciously] keep track of such large numbers during performances, and for that reason, it is particularly important that we do not attempt to connect an alpha-numeric symbol directly to the perceived musical aesthetic.[27] Rather, alpha-numeric symbolism is to be regarded as a kind of occult aesthetic. Whereas pure-number symbols take their meanings from direct association with extra-musical objects or ideas, alpha-numeric symbolism simply equates letters of the alphabet with integers. Nevertheless, it is clear that groups of alphabetically encoded numbers can be employed to stand for specific words.

Although an alpha-numeric symbol is similar to a note-name symbol in regard to the clarity of its reference, there is one important difference between the two; whereas it is possible to prove beyond any reasonable doubt that Bach employed note-name symbolism in *The Art of Fugue,* we cannot be absolutely certain that he used either alpha-numeric or pure-number symbols.

At this point, it is imperative that we distance ourselves from the grotesque speculation about alpha-numeric symbolism which runs rampant in many treatises on Bach. Nevertheless, alpha-numeric symbolism cannot be com-

---

[26] In the *alpha-numeric* system employed by Bach, the letter pair "I /J" was represented by a single number, as was the letter pair "U/V." That is, I/J = 9; U/V = 20.

[27] This remains true, even though the musical materials may actually be directly computed by the alpha-numeric method.

pletely eliminated from our discussion. In fact, it is quite possible that Bach actually did employ both alpha-numeric and pure-numeric symbolism in *The Art of Fugue*. There is good evidence for Bach's use of alpha-numeric symbols, particularly if we consider his penchant for using them as references to himself. In a number of Bach's compositions, musical materials constructed from fourteen, forty-one, and (less often) one hundred fifty-eight elements appear with astounding frequency in exposed places. We must admit, however, that even if these spots do contain such references to Bach, they might be significant only for the composer himself.

It is possible, however, that the second subject with its forty-one pitches is more than just an alpha-numeric reference to the name "J.S. BACH." This symbolic reference to the composer could also be viewed as a preparation for the unequivocal "BACH," which appears in note-name symbols at the beginning of the third subject. Though this relationship is pure conjecture, I wish to stress again that my interpretation does not regard any symbolic reference to "Bach" in *The Art of Fugue* simply to mean: "I have composed this." Instead, the forty-one pitches contained in the restless second subject might well express the thought: "I, J.S. Bach, am the one who is running toward the goal, though I am yet living an imperfect human existence *(Dasein)*." Because of a possible connection between the alpha-numeric symbol (forty-one) and the restless motion of the second subject, I shall consider the second subject of the closing fugue to be a musical representation of Bach's goal-directed, but human, existence. In addition, both the alpha-numeric reference to J.S. Bach and the restless character of the second subject provide a strong motivational impetus for the B-A-C-H-C♯-D theme.

The "peaceful" first subject and the "restless" second subject might also share a pure-number symbolic connection. Whereas the first subject of the closing fugue is seven pitches long, the second subject, constructed from forty-one pitches, is seven measures long.

It should also be noted that Bach consistently employs stepwise chromatic motion in those voices which accompany the "running" theme; this chromatic motion is maintained at the point where the first and second subjects are combined for the first time (Ex. 11).[28]

It is only during the third part of the closing fugue, however, that a true countersubject actually appears (Ex. 12). Here, the ascending half step from the discant clausula at the end of the first subject [measures 196-97, tenor] continues chromatically upward (d♯-e) to form the beginning of this joyfully stirring countersubject.

---

[28] [Translator's note: The author interprets chromatic space in *The Art of Fugue* to represent "human frailty" *(Dasein)*. See chapter 1, p.9.]

EXAMPLE 11

Closing Fugue

Second Subject

First Subject

stepwise chromatic motion

EXAMPLE 12

Closing Fugue: beginning of the third exposition

Answer

alto   194

tenor

B-A-C-H-C♯-D Theme (Third Subject)

discant clausula   chromatic continuation of the discant clausula

Countersubject

Subject

(soprano)

Countersubject

Countersubject

Countersubject

3

The Last Seven Measures of the Closing Fugue

I n order to summarize our earlier observations, provide an overview, and enlarge upon certain details, we shall now return to the passage where our discussion began— the last seven measures of the closing fugue. These last seven measures can be considered the nuclear center of the entire closing fugue, if we simply substitute the ground theme for the extant "contrapuntally free" soprano (see the supranotated line in Ex. 1). This fragmentary passage also provides us a model of Bach's compositional processes, and a starting place from which we can trace the influence of all the thematic materials contained in the closing fugue.

The second subject (alto) and the third subject (tenor) act as counter-themes to the first subject (bass). As we discussed earlier, the first closing-fugue subject is derived from the initial four pitches of the ground theme.[1] Similarly, the second subject is related to the eighth-note rhythmic motion at the end of the ground theme;[2] the third subject (the B-A-C-H-C♯-D theme) is generated from the half-step motive which occurs at the midpoint of the ground theme.[3]

Each of these three "new themes" distinctly projects the specific materials of the location in the ground theme from which it was derived [beginning, middle, or end].[4] The three extant closing-fugue subjects illustrate, respectively, specific latent developmental possibilities contained in the materials of the ground theme: pure diatonicism, forward-driving rhythmic motion, and chromaticism. Since the ground theme was apparently planned to be the fourth [and

---

[1] Both the first four pitches of the ground theme and the entire first closing-fugue subject outline the tonic triad (d-f-a). See chapter 2, pp.13-14.

[2] See chapter 2, pp.21-22.

[3] Both the normal and inverted forms of the ground theme are required to derive the B-A-C-H-C♯-D theme. See chapter 1, p.11.

final] subject of the closing fugue, it can be regarded, simultaneously, as both the material source for and a synthesis of the three other closing-fugue subjects.

It was possible for Bach to plan a lengthy and diversified single fugue from the materials of four separate fugues for two reasons: 1) all of the closing-fugue subjects are materially related to the ground theme; and 2) each of the four subjects has a unique musical structure and shape. Had Bach lived to complete the fugue, the distinctive structure of the subjects would have certainly made it possible for the ear to recognize each of them at the point where they were all brought together. We must not focus solely on the unique musical shape and structure of each subject, however. It is also vital that we recognize and consider the aesthetic individuality of the four closing-fugue subjects.

If we accept the theory that Bach actually intended the closing fugue to be a quadruple fugue, a true Baroque "rhetorical moment" would have certainly taken place at the point where all four subjects appeared together. The extant last seven measures clearly show how the various expressive elements, established throughout the course of the entire movement, were designed to contrapuntally fit with each other. In this passage, we encounter the first subject (constructed only from perfect fifths and major seconds) functioning simultaneously as both the fundamental bass and a *cantus firmus*; its symmetrical form and triad-derived pitch structure convey a sense of "internal repose." Here also is the second subject, which seems to "run" toward its goal, and the third subject (B-A-C-H-C♯-D theme) with its intense half-step motives. Finally, Example 1 shows that the ground theme, which musically represents the work as a whole, also fits this contrapuntal texture.

If our interpretation is applied to this spot, the meaning of this thematic convergence becomes quite clear— the B-A-C-H-C♯-D theme actively exhibits the difference between "imperfect human nature" and the "perfect nature of God." Moreover, the B-A-C-H-C♯-D theme also symbolizes within itself the desire for unification with God.[5] We have already discussed how the "human condition," the "nature of God," and the human desire for unification with the Creator are symbolically represented in the "restful" first theme and the "run-

---

4 [Translator's note: Though the author uses the term "new theme" (author's quotation marks), he does not imply that any of these subjects are independently conceived. Rather, these subjects should be considered thematic metamorphoses of the ground theme, in spite of their unrelated ("new") surface appearance. (Thematic metamorphosis will be discussed further in chapter 8.) The use of the term "new theme" here may also be a gentle reproof of those analysts who have missed the musical connections between the ground theme and those thematic materials in *The Art of Fugue* which appear to be independent, but in fact find their genesis in the materials of the ground theme.]

5 [Translator's note: The chromatically derived pitches, b-a-c-h, represent Bach's "imperfect human condition" (*Dasein*), the tonic pitch (d) stands for the "Ground of Being" (*Sein*), and the double discant clausula (c♯-d/c♯-d) portrays the emphatic desire for unity between the two. See chapter 1, pp.6-10.]

ning" second theme.[6] The ground theme has been a "self-contained" structure since the very beginning of the work; it symbolically represents the source from which everything is derived and to which everything finally returns.[7]

In addition to the possible pure-numeric symbolism associated with the first and second subjects,[8] it is also possible to detect alpha-numeric symbolism in the materials of the last seven measures of the closing fugue. The second subject retains its forty-one pitch length here, but only if its initial eighth note (e) is disregarded. We will consider this initial e to be an extra, nonthematic pitch, since it functions primarily to introduce eighth-note motion smoothly into the measure and to produce a consonant pitch in the soprano (quarter-note c♯).[9] In the final seven measures, both the pure-numeric and the alpha-numeric symbols (connected with the first two subjects) become contrapuntally associated with the note-name symbolism which occurs in the third subject. An intentional meaning is strongly implied here, since all of these extramusical symbols also seem to fit the aesthetic character of the subjects with which they are connected.

The psychology of the creative process might be able to provide us a reason why Bach chose this place in the closing fugue as a stopping point.[10] As has been pointed out, this seven-measure section is not only the spot in the work where the three "new" subjects are first brought together, but it is also the place where the ground theme can be contrapuntally combined with the three other subjects. Before interrupting his work on the closing fugue, it seems reasonable that Bach would have desired to reach the point where all these subjects could be united. His obituary (*Nekrolog*) seems to indicate that he had no notion of his impending death, since it states that the composer, up to the time of his eye surgery, possessed "an otherwise thoroughly healthy constitution."

Recent research indicates that Bach could have actually started work on *The Art of Fugue* in the late 1730's.[11] Though expressions of death often appear more

---

[6] [Translator's note: For a complete discussion of the symbolic nature of the first and second subjects of the closing fugue see chapter 2, especially pp.13-15 and pp.20-22, respectively.]

[7] [Translator's note: For a more complete discussion of the ground theme and its significance, see chapter 5.]

[8] The first subject contains seven pitches; the second subject is contained in seven measures.

[9] [Translator's note: This soprano c♯ [measure 233, beat one], appears in the last seven measures of the incomplete third section of the closing fugue. If the ground theme is hypothetically substituted for the soprano voice, however, the c♯ would no longer be present, and is therefore, bracketed [ ] in Ex. 1.]

[10] Bach's autograph of the closing fugue is a fair copy written on two staves (BWV 1080:19) from which the four-stave, open-score version was later constructed. [Translator's note: See footnote[1] in the Author's Preface.]

[11] The dates of origin for *The Art of Fugue* will be briefly discussed in chapter 9 (see p.108).

pronounced during the period of a composer's [terminal] illness, the closing fugue does not seem to be any more concerned with such expressions than the rest of the work. Rather, the closing fugue follows the same basic patterns established by Bach's other late works and by his philosophy of art and life in general.

There are so many riddles to solve that it is difficult to even begin discussing how the closing fugue should have been completed. However, I believe that the remarks made by C.P.E. and the obituary (*Nekrolog*) written by Johann Friedrich Agricola are clear and trustworthy.[12] Furthermore, there is little doubt that someone in J.S. Bach's acquaintance must have had an understanding of the complete plan of the closing fugue. It is also conceivable that someone might have even been given a complete draft, in which the closing fugue was developed all the way to its conclusion. If such a draft actually existed, it would have probably appeared similar in format to the surviving autograph fragment.[13]

Bach's obituary further states that terminal illness hindered the composer's progress in "completing the draft of the penultimate fugue as well as working out the final fugue." The latter was to have "contained four themes, requiring note-for-note inversion in all four voices." As has already been pointed out, it is certainly possible to consider each of the four sections of the closing fugue as an individual fugue. Since Agricola understood the closing fugue to consist of four separate fugues, it is quite possible that the "penultimate" fugue, mentioned in the obituary, is none other than the incomplete third section of the closing fugue. Furthermore, it is all but certain that the ground theme was to have entered as the fourth subject of the "final" fugue. Had the "final" mirror fugue actually been completed, it would have probably been analogous in its fugal design to Contrapunctus XII and XIII.[14]

Assuming that *The Art of Fugue* was intended to be completed in the manner we have discussed, the closing fugue would have actually brought together, one last time, all of the fugal types employed in the entire work. The first section of the closing fugue contains an example of a fugue on one subject, but directly

---

12 [Translator's note: Agricola (1720-74) studied music with J.S. Bach while a law student at the University of Leipzig. He was appointed court composer to King Frederick the Great of Prussia in 1751. It was Agricola who wrote Bach's obituary (*Nekrolog*) in 1754 for Lorenz Mizler's monthly musical periodical, *Neu eröffnete musikalische Bibliothek*. The complete text of the *Nekrolog* can be found in: *Bach-Dokumente,* ed. Bach-Archiv Leipzig (Kassel: Bärenreiter Verlag, 1972), 3: 80-93.]

13 [Translator's note: BWV 1080:19.]

14 [Translator's note: The numbering of all the Contrapuncti will follow the author's suggestions, which are fully discussed in chapter 9. For quick reference to his ordering scheme see: Table 2, p.114.]

following the exposition, the contrapuntal techniques of inversion and stretto are also presented.[15] The following three sections of the closing fugue contain fugues on multiple subjects; that is, fugues on two, three, and four subjects, respectively.

According to Bach's obituary, the "final fugue" was planned as a mirror fugue.[16] The technique of note-for-note mirroring, the "crowning glory" of fugal art, had already brought the work's progression of contrapuntal techniques to its zenith in Contrapuncti XII and XIII. Bach, however, had apparently planned to employ mirror-fugue technique one last time in *The Art of Fugue*. It is quite certain that he intended to bring the entire work to a close with yet another mirror fugue in the fourth and final section of the closing fugue.

A musical composition that is completely mirror invertible exists in two separate states. One is created by the original compositional form of the piece and the other by its inversion. These two separate states can also be considered as symbols. The two fugues of a mirror-invertible pair are totally different from each other, but are also completely contained in one another. The musical phenomenon is such that neither one of the fugues in a mirror pair trespasses on the ground of the other. The mutually exclusive yet highly interdependent relationship between the members of a mirror-fugue pair is not unlike the Lutheran understanding of the relationship between the redeemed "human creation" and the "Creator." Moreover, this state of redemption is not considered to depend upon human works, but it proceeds directly out of the Creator's mercy. A mirror fugue can thus be considered a symbol which represents an effortless transfer of security from one member of the pair to the other. Therefore, the mirror fugues in *The Art of Fugue,* including the one planned for the "final" fugue, could actually be symbolic of the Christian doctrine of "salvation by grace."

---

[15] [Translator's note: The technique of inversion is representative of the work's three counter fugues (Contrapunctus V, VI, and VII) and the technique of stretto is associated with the four double fugues (Contrapunctus VIII, IX, X, and XI). See Table 2, p.114.]

[16] [Translator's note: A mirror fugue is a fugue in which all of the musical materials can be inverted to form a contrapuntally correct but completely separate fugue; i.e., intervals that are inflected upward in the original fugue become inflected downward by the exact same factor in the mirror fugue and vice versa. Furthermore, mirror fugues are often constructed so that the voices of the two fugues will trade positions relative to one another (e.g., the top voice of the original fugue becomes the bottom voice in the inverted fugue, etc.).]

4

The Chorale

I t was impossible to publish an unfinished musical composition during the time of Bach. Probably for that reason, the last seven measures of the closing fugue were omitted from the first printed edition of *The Art of Fugue* and replaced with Bach's organ chorale, *Wenn wir in höchsten Nöten sein*. Moreover, it is all but certain that C.P.E. was responsible for concluding the work in this fashion. It only takes a glance at the external features of this G-major organ chorale to see that it has no musical connection whatever to *The Art of Fugue*.[1] Indeed, numerous critical articles have confirmed that this chorale arrangement has no direct relationship to the cycle. Another question remains unanswered, however; how and why did this organ chorale come to be associated with *The Art of Fugue*?

I am including a discussion of the chorale here because its text and materials seem to share some of the same rhetorical concepts and spiritual allusions that have become the thesis of our study. Although I will use the traditional association of this chorale with *The Art of Fugue* in order to help clarify my interpretation, it should be remembered that the chorale does not really belong to the work at all.

The preface, located on the title page overleaf of the first printed copies of *The Art of Fugue*,[2] carries a statement that Bach "extemporaneously dictated [the chorale] to one of his friends during his blindness."[3] This same report was then adopted word for word by Friedrich Wilhelm Marpurg in his 1752 preface to the

---

[1] Features like the origins of the piece, its setting, formal type, and specific compositional techniques.

[2] Presumably written by C.P.E.

[3] Forkel also made the claim that "Bach dictated the chorale to his son-in-law [Johann Christoph] Altnikol only a few days before the composer's death." [Translator's note: see Johann Nickolaus Forkel, *Über Johann Sebastian Bachs Leben, Kunst and Kunstwerke* (Leipzig, 1802; reprinted East Berlin: Henschelverlag und Gesellschaft, 1968): 95.]

work. The reliability of this account is somewhat questionable, however, since C.P.E. failed to mention his own firmly established absence from Leipzig during and directly before the time of his father's death.

The act of extemporaneous musical dictation might seem a little less mysterious if we assume that a keyboard instrument was used in the process. Furthermore, Bach had written earlier versions of this same organ chorale and it is somewhat doubtful that the version attached to *The Art of Fugue* was actually the dictated ["deathbed"] chorale. Nevertheless, if the report concerning the "extemporaneous dictation" is accurate, that undertaking certainly would have been one of Bach's last musical activities. Moreover, it would have taken place when the composer was in rapidly failing health and totally blind.

In addition to the chorale setting attached to *The Art of Fugue,* we know that Bach composed two other organ chorales on the same tune.[4] The earliest version is found in the *Orgelbüchlein* collection from Bach's Weimar period (1708-1717) and is entitled *Wenn wir in höchsten Nöten sein* [BWV 641]. In this setting, the chorale tune appears heavily ornamented in the uppermost voice, and it is stated in its entirety, without any accompanying interludes between the phrases by the lower three voices. Instead, the lower voices provide the melody with a polyphonic accompaniment based on imitative entries of the chorale's opening motive.

The second known setting, which bears the same title, is the one that was attached to the first printed edition of *The Art of Fugue.*[5] Bach seems to have transferred all four phrases of the melody from the arrangement found in the *Orgelbüchlein* directly into this second setting without any significant changes in the chorale's structural pitches. This time, however, the melody appears in a much less ornamented form, and its individual phrases are introduced one at a time, by means of fughetta-like interludes.[6] The subjects of these fughetta interludes are based, respectively, on the opening motive of each phrase of the melody.

The third and last known arrangement of this chorale is found at the end of the group of Bach's late organ compositions known today as *The Leipzig Original Manuscript Collection.* It is well established that Bach was busy during the final years of his life, revising and making fair copies of the works in this collection. The first part contains six trio sonatas [BWV 525-30], and the second

---

[4] From this point, we will assume that C.P.E. Bach was the person responsible for attaching of the chorale to the fugue cycle.

[5] *Wenn wir in höchsten Nöten sein.* Unfortunately, J.S. Bach's autograph manuscript for this version of the chorale is lost.

[6] Fughetta-like interludes are regularly found in Pachelbel's organ chorales. [Translator's note: A fughetta is a short fugue-like texture employed within a larger work. A fughetta often consists only of a fugal exposition, where the voices first enter in turn.]

part, seventeen chorale arrangements [BWV 651-67].[7] These chorales are immediately followed by a set of canonic variations on the Christmas chorale *Vom Himmel hoch, da komm ich her* [BWV 769]. Directly after this set of variations comes a fair copy of the organ chorale in question, though the setting is not in Bach's hand. Moreover, the entire last page is missing. Entitled *Vor deinen Thron tret' ich* [BWV 668], this version is similar in style, but far superior to the chorale version attached to *The Art of Fugue*.[8]

The organ chorale appended to *The Art of Fugue* was probably not the dictated chorale, but an earlier setting. During the time that Bach was producing the revisions and fair copies of the organ chorales, it is quite likely that he wrote out, on a single sheet, a preliminary draft version of what would later become *Vor deinen Thron tret' ich*.[9] It is altogether possible that C.P.E. happened upon this draft and chose it to complete *The Art of Fugue*, without knowing about the better subsequent version that was copied into the *Leipzig Collection*.[10] This means that the "dictation" version of the chorale might possibly be the fair-copy entry at the end of the *Leipzig Collection*, rather than the setting which was attached to *The Art of Fugue*. It was certainly reported to C.P.E. that his father had dictated a chorale on his deathbed; and not knowing exactly what his father had actually done, he might have assumed that the chorale version in his possession was that dictation. It is not impossible that C.P.E. then decided to solve the problem of the unfinished closing fugue by simply attaching the chorale version at hand. Had C.P.E. known the later better version of the chorale, he would have undoubtedly chosen it instead. Thus, the organ chorale *Vor deinen Thron . . .*, found at the end of the *Leipzig Collection*, actually could have been the chorale that should have been appended to *The Art of Fugue*.

The question remains, however, why Bach had this organ chorale copied into the manuscript collection at all. In defense of the myth surrounding Bach's "deathbed chorale," we can simply argue that from the earliest times, this late entry has been used as evidence of Bach's interest in continuing and enlarging the *Leipzig Collection*. Did Bach, however, really work on these manuscripts during the time that he was totally blind and terminally ill? Evidence to the contrary is provided in the following four points:

---

[7] These seventeen chorales represent different types and styles of organ chorales.

[8] [Translator's note: Hymnals in the German Evangelical Church (Lutheran) employ the same tune for both *Wenn wir in höchsten Nöten sein* and *Vor deinen Thron tret' ich hiermit*. Therefore, general analytical comments pertaining to the melody of one of these texts will also apply to the other.]

[9] [Translator's note: Since the chorale attached to the first printed edition of the cycle was entitled *Wenn wir in höchsten Nöten sein*, the supposed draft used by C.P.E. could not have carried the title *Vor deinen Thron tret' ich*.]

[10] After Bach's death, the *Leipzig Collection* of autograph manuscripts was probably at first in the possession of the composer's son, Wilhelm Friedemann Bach.

1) Placing the chorale at the end of the *Leipzig Collection,* after the canonic variations on *Vom Himmel hoch,* fails to show a logically motivated continuity within the collection. This is especially true if we consider that a chorale in the "Pachelbel style" *(Nun danket alle Gott)* was already represented in the collection.

2) A basic conflict occurs between the changing imitative subjects which introduce each new chorale phrase and the main contrapuntal subject which is retained throughout. This conflict pervades the entire chorale, but such internal opposition is not typical of the collection as a whole.

3) The change of title from *Wenn wir in höchsten nöten sein* to *Vor deinen Thron tret' ich hiermit* can only be explained in terms of the text's relationship to a specific event or occasion. The adoption of the latter title is evidence that Bach had a particular purpose in mind for this setting.

4) In the time of Bach, the text of *Vor deinen Thron . . .* functioned primarily as an evensong chorale because of the line *Drum dank ich dir mit Herz und Mund/ O Gott! in dieser Abendstund* (Therefore I thank thee with heart and voice/ O God, in this evening hour).[11] Bach certainly could have employed this text as a chorale on death, however, especially if we examine the first and last verses:

First Verse	**Last Verse**
Vor deinen Thron tret ich hiermit,	*Ein selig Ende mir bescher,*
I come before Thy throne,	Bestow upon me a blessed end,
	Am jüngsten Tag erwecke mich,
O Gott und dich demütig bitt:	Awake me on Judgement Day,
O God, and humbly beseech Thee:	
	Herr, daß ich dich schau ewiglich:
Wend dein genädig Angesicht	that I might look eternally on Thee,
turn not your merciful countenance	O Lord:
Von mir betrübtem Sünder nicht.	*Amen, Amen, erhöre mich!"*
away from this miserable sinner.	Amen, Amen, hear my voice!

---

[11] From verse eleven. [Translator's note: The word *Abendstund* (evening hour) has not continued to be universally used in more modern German hymnals. The word *Morgenstund* (morning hour) is found (substituted?) in both in the nineteenth-century *Mechlenburgisches Kirchengesangbuch* (1868) and in the recent *Evangelisches Gesangbuch* (Niedersachsen, 1986).]

This chorale text, with its fifteen stanzas, portrays the very quintessence of the Christian faith and the Christian understanding of the relationship between "human sinfulness" and "a perfect God."[12] Furthermore, Bach would certainly have understood either the specific or the more general interpretation of this text; that is, he would have understood its fundamental message, whether it was applied to the evening of a particular day or life, or to the evening of every day and every life.

Though Bach had this chorale copied into the *Leipzig Collection,* it is out of sequence with others of its type; and because the chorale stands alone at the end, it functions as a kind of epilogue to the collection. Symbolically, it is as if Bach desired to close this collection of chorales by placing the entire group of manuscripts under the message of faith expressed by *Vor deinen Thron tret' ich.* Except for the composer's private reasons, one finds it difficult to imagine why Bach would have wanted to include this piece in the *Leipzig Collection* at all. If I may be allowed to speculate, it seems as if this piece is a compositional prayer, uttered in the medium of an organ chorale, and it is possible that Bach combined his artistic knowledge of the organ with the clear textual message of the chorale in order to musically share an aspect of his personal faith with the entire Christian community.[13]

Indeed, this (dictated?) chorale contains within it strong evidence of Bach's belief in God, and it is this aspect of the piece that emerges more important than its objective purposes, musical expression, or public intent. The chorale reveals far more than its immediate reason for existence; it also exhibits the strong personal faith behind Bach's life and creative identity. It is as if Bach were saying: "God is the reference point of my life, and though I am a wretched human being, I am united to Him through the mercy of Christ"—*"Gott Sohn! du hast mich durch dein Blut/ Erlöset von der Höllenglut"* [Son of God! through your blood, Thou hast saved me from the fires of hell].[14]

For the moment, we shall accept that C.P.E. would have been at least partially correct in attaching the chorale from the *Leipzig Collection* to *The Art of Fugue.* If we further accept the possibility that this chorale also contains a basic statement of the composer's faith, then we have in this "musical prayer," a better explanation of Bach's life and creative motivation than is found in any other document. There certainly would have been some merit in choosing this chorale to serve as an epilogue to *The Art of Fugue,* if for no other reason than that it was written during the same time as Bach's last efforts on this cycle of

---

12 [Translator's note: Many modern German hymnbooks do not include all of the original fifteen verses.]

13 The organ was the instrument on which Bach began his career as a performer and composer.

14 [Translator's note: From verse five of *Vor deinen Thron tret' ich hiermit.*]

fugues and canons. Insertion of the chorale at the end of the closing fugue, however, not only provided the work with a conclusion, but it also placed the aesthetic meaning of the entire cycle under the fundamental textual statement of the chorale.

Once again, it is necessary to stress the point that this chorale actually has little or nothing to do with the cycle. Nevertheless, an understanding of its inner processes might provide us with further insight as we attempt to interpret the meaning of *The Art of Fugue*. It is important that we consider the chorale because it seems to make the same fundamental assertion about the "human condition" that seems to be symbolized in the cycle's musical materials and compositional techniques. From this point on, we shall only discuss the chorale in order to document the importance of the expressive content that it shares with *The Art of Fugue*.

It is a far more complex process to analyze meaning in *The Art of Fugue* than it is in the chorale. Starting with the message implied in the B-A-C-H-C♯-D theme, and without making any reference to the chorale, we have developed an interpretation which supports a concrete statement of faith. Instead of being associated with text, the fundamental message of the work is presented in an instrumental idiom which is tied to the specific musical materials used in the construction of fugue subjects. We have attempted to describe the meaning of the two sides of this statement by using the terms *Dasein* and *Sein,* which, respectively, represent the "human condition" and the "nature of God."

Although the chorale cannot be used as a proof that Bach was setting forth a similar message in *The Art of Fugue,* it can be used as evidence to support that theory. Nevertheless, the problem remains: appending the chorale to *The Art of Fugue* was still just an attempt to complete the cycle with a movement that does not share the same musical materials. Today, we can hardly understand the reasons why it was necessary to attach the chorale to the work at all.

In fact, the whole question of including the chorale in the cycle is somewhat perplexing. Forkel's biography states that the chorale expresses "pious submission and devotion . . . [and is] deeply moving." We know, however, that the chorale is totally independent of *The Art of Fugue.* Furthermore, the chorale contains a much less comprehensive and totally superfluous repetition of the message that has already been proclaimed from within *The Art of Fugue* itself. It is totally unnecessary to attach the chorale to the end of the closing fugue in order for us to grasp Bach's intended meaning in the "final" mirror fugue or to understand the underlying message of the entire work. The text lines *"Du hast mich, o Gott! Vater mild/Gemacht zu deinem Ebenbild"* [You have made me into your/ likeness, O God, gentle Father!] are not needed at all.[15] The statement

---

15 [Translator's note: From verse two of *Vor deinen Thron tret' ich hiermit.*]

carried in the musical materials of the cycle stands complete in itself, and though the attached chorale may help clarify the basic statement of the preceding work, it is in no way required for an understanding of *The Art of Fugue.*

Possible Alpha-numeric Symbolism in the Chorales

To close this part of our discussion, I shall briefly cite several possible alpha-numeric symbols that occur in the organ chorales discussed in this chapter. It should be remembered, however, that what I have to say here is only ancillary to our study of *The Art of Fugue.*

It may not be simply happenstance that the highly ornamented uppermost voice of the *Orgelbüchlein* chorale, *Wenn wir in höchsten Nöten sein* [BWV 641], contains 158 notes. Instead, it is quite possible that these notes could be an alpha-numerical symbol which stands for the composer's full name, "Johann Sebastian Bach."[16] From this possible self-reference, we might come to the conclusion that Bach had a very personal relationship to this particular text, a probability which increases if we examine both the version of the chorale used to close *The Art of Fugue* and the setting found in the *Leipzig Collection* [BWV 668]. In all published chorale books, the first phrase of the tune *Wenn wir in höchsten Nöten sein* contains eleven pitches. However, in the first phrase of the chorale which closes *The Art of Fugue* and in the chorale found in the *Leipzig Collection,* Bach added three extra notes to the melody. The insertion of these tones, which appear to be little more than ornaments, brings to fourteen the total number of notes contained in these first phrases. Fourteen corresponds to the alpha-numeric value of the name "Bach."

The complete tune, as it is represented in period Baroque-era hymnals, is thirty-six pitches long. If this basic chorale tune is compared to the melody of the same two later organ chorales, however, one can see that Bach also added extra ornamentation to the third and fourth phrases of the later organ works. With the addition of these inserted tones, Bach increased the total number of notes in the entire melody to forty-one. The number forty-one corresponds to the alpha-numeric value of the name "J.S. Bach."

If we remove the ornamental pitches from the melody of the *Orgelbüchlein* arrangement, upon which Bach apparently based the two later organ arrangements in question, it becomes clear that the five additional melody notes found in the two later chorales are not a part of the background melodic structure of the *Orgelbüchlein* version. It is, therefore, strongly implied that Bach intentionally added the five extra tones. Moreover, this could also be further evidence that the 158 melody notes in the *Orgelbüchlein* chorale might not have appeared there

16 [Translator's note: For a discussion of alpha-numeric symbolism see: chapter 2, pp.22-24.]

merely by chance. Thus, it is entirely possible that Bach borrowed both the concept of alpha-numeric symbolism as well as the basic melodic structure from the *Orgelbüchlein* version when he composed the two later chorales.

Is it really only by chance that these exact numbers of notes appear in the chorale tune? Could Bach have actually connected his name, via alpha-numeric symbolism, to the melody of the *Leipzig Collection* chorale for the same reason that he connected his name, via note-name symbolism, to the last "new" subject of the closing fugue in *The Art of Fugue?* The connection of the name "Bach" with the musical materials seems to imply the same meaning in both works. The emphatic "reaching for tonic," characteristic of the B-A-C-H motto and its attached double discant clausula, is analogous to the symbolic connection between the chorale melody's forty-one pitches and its underlying text.

5

The Ground Theme

At first glance, it appears as if there is nothing particularly remarkable about the ground theme (Ex. 13). Nevertheless, I am constantly amazed, even after many sessions of score study, by the staggering amount of musical material that Bach forged from this subject. In fact, these insignificant appearing twelve pitches identify, describe, and establish the entire gamut of compositional possibilities in *The Art of Fugue*.

EXAMPLE 13

The Ground Theme: Contrapunctus I

The four tonic pitches of the Ground Theme

The ground theme is important for several reasons: 1) it is itself a suitable fugue subject, complete with numerous inherent capabilities of variation and development; 2) it contains within it the potential for extensive contrapuntal manipulation; 3) it contains the basic melodic gestures which initiate the work's contrasting diatonic and chromatic materials, which form the B-A-C-H motto, and which generate many of the basic formative concepts that are applied to the fugues and canons throughout the entire work;[1] and 4) according to our interpretation, the ground theme also carries a rhetorical message.

---

[1] These melodic gestures not only provide the point of origin for technical aspects found throughout the work, but are also the source of rhetorical characterization for all the fugues and canons. We have already discussed in rudimentary fashion how the thematic materials of the closing fugue are related to the ground theme. [Translator's note: For a discussion of these derivations see chapter 1, p.4 (closing fugue's third subject); chapter 2, p.13 (closing fugue's first subject); chapter 2, p.20 (closing fugue's second subject).]

The creative and material-generating power of the ground theme can only be explained if we conclude that Bach carefully planned this subject in advance. Since he introduces all of its possibilities of inversion and variation during the course of *The Art of Fugue,* Bach must have consciously chosen the cycle's technical and contrapuntal requirements before beginning the process of working out the individual movements. Furthermore, while listening to, playing and studying the entire work, one perceives a continuous ebb and flow between the strong presence of the ground theme and the coming and going of other compositional events. From this point on, we shall attempt to determine how Bach accomplished this essential ebb and flow. The discussion which follows will take us inside the work to those spots that might help us to better understand the musical materials of the cycle and what they represent.

The Art of Fugue is an incomparable example of monothematicism. Therefore, a study of its ground theme is vital to an understanding of the entire work. Unfortunately, our interpretation does not make it any easier to understand the compositional structure of this theme or its rhetorical character.

The Pitch D

D minor is the key not only of the ground theme, but also the key of every canon and fugue in the entire cycle. Furthermore, the tonic pitch d presents a fixed point of reference for all melodic motion, chord progression, tonicization,[2] and modulation in *The Art of Fugue.* The tone d occurs no less than four times within the ground theme itself. It not only provides the ground theme with its first and last pitches, but it also surrounds the leading tone (c♯) at the midpoint of the theme (Ex. 13).

The ground theme exhibits a cyclical structure in which both the pitches d and f play a part.[3] The arches in Ex. 14 show the quasi-symmetrical construction of the ground theme and its axis of symmetry around the pitch c♯. The ground theme is not perfectly symmetrical for several reasons, however: 1) the note a, near the beginning of the theme, does not take part in the pitch symmetry; 2) the rhythmic values of the symmetrically identified pitches are not

---

[2] [Translator's note: The German musical term *Ausweichung,* translated here as "tonicization," relates to the technical procedure of temporarily replacing the tonic with another tone of the scale. Tonicization is often accomplished by the use of secondary-dominant or secondary-subdominant sonorities and is not considered true modulation, since the original tonal center is quickly reestablished. Modulation is generally considered a longer-term change of tonal center, where the original tonic is not immediately reestablished.]

[3] [Translator's note: The term "cyclical" is used here to describe a compositional technique where musical elements which appear in later sections or movements are the same or similar to those appearing earlier.]

the same on both sides of the central axis, and, most important; 3) the implied symmetry consists of a progression of tonic pitches that are not of equal weight or importance.[4]

EXAMPLE 14

Arch-like symmetry in the Ground Theme: Contrapunctus I

As we shall discuss later, the pitch c# will be enlarged and projected into the overall plan of *The Art of Fugue* as the axis of symmetry for the entire work.[5] We shall also discuss how the symmetrical plan of the work is superimposed on a progressive order of fugal complexity; that is, we shall see how the work begins with those types of fugues that contain the simplest devices and ends with those that are most complex.

In our discussion of the closing fugue (chapter 1), we already mentioned the large formal symmetry of the work. We saw that the final quadruple fugue could be considered a symmetrical counterpart to the opening group of four fugues. Moreover, the [planned] reentry of the ground theme at the end the closing fugue would have also supplied a pole of symmetry in the work that could be traced all the way back to its initial entrance at the very beginning of the work. At the same time, however, the [planned] mirror fugue on four subjects (section four of the closing fugue) would have served as a climax to the ongoing progression of contrapuntal techniques.

The Key of D Minor

Why did Bach choose the key of d minor for *The Art of Fugue*? One possible explanation concerns the Baroque-era practice of matching individual keys to specific affections.

---

[4] The first d is the starting pitch; the second d appears after the line has progressed through the fifth and third above; the third d follows the leading tone c#. The leading tone resolution before the third d actually defines it as tonic for the first time, while the quarter-note motion of the resolution releases the line to again move forward. The final d is the goal pitch which is preceded by the initiation of rhythmic motion in eighth notes. Although the final d concludes the ground theme, it also tends to launch the composition forward at the same time. The final d of the ground theme is of variable duration throughout the work and it signals both the entrance of the fugal answer and the commencement of the counterpoint against the answer.

[5] [Translator's note: For a detailed discussion of symmetry in the complete work see chapter 9.]

Baroque music theorist Johannes Mattheson (1681-1764) provides us with some perspective on this topic. He claims that the key of d minor, which is based on the structure of a modal scale associated with traditional church music [Dorian mode], conveys a musical character that is "somewhat devout and peaceful, as well as somewhat spacious, pleasant and contented. This same mode implies prayerful devotion in matters of the church, but it is also capable of conveying calmness in matters of the ordinary life. Though no edifying possibility is excluded, this mode is certainly better employed with flowing musical textures rather than ones that are angular."[6]

Doubtless, Mattheson's ideas have some validity, even for *The Art of Fugue,* but it is impossible to go any further with his characterization of keys. His discussion is far too general to be of much use in this study, and his statements are overly biased toward the emotional. Moreover, he describes the affections associated with the various keys without providing any explanation as to how or why the keys tend to produce them. Therefore, Mattheson's study of key affections cannot be directly applied to *The Art of Fugue.*

We shall now examine an aspect of d minor which may actually have provided a basis for Bach's choice of key, and examine how the key of d minor fits our interpretation.

The pitch d distinguishes itself from all other pitches in that it is the center of intervallic symmetry in the pure-diatonic scale system [no sharps or flats]. In Example 15, the whole note d is shown as the midpoint of the white notes on the keyboard. As we move away step by step from this central pitch, the same succession of whole steps (⌐) and half steps (∧) is maintained in both ascending and descending directions. If we begin a pure-diatonic scale on the pitch d the Dorian mode is formed.

EXAMPLE 15

Retrograde symmetry of intervals in the Dorian Mode

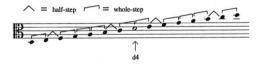

It is conceivable that Bach chose the key of d minor for *The Art of Fugue* because d is the symmetrical center of the diatonic system. Furthermore, because of this special position, it is also possible that Bach could have intended the pitch d to symbolically represent the order of God (*Seinsordnung*). If we follow this

---

6 See the section entitled *Von der musicalischen Tohne Eigenschafft und Würckung in Ausdrückung der Affecten* [On the Quality of Musical Tones and their Influence on the Expression of Affections] in Johannes Mattheson, *Das Neu-Eröffnete Orchestre* (Hamburg, 1713).

interpretation further, d can be viewed as the "Tonic" from which everything proceeds and to which everything returns.[7] The quasi-symmetrical pattern produced by the four tonic pitches in the ground theme (Ex. 14) provides evidence for this interpretation, and we have already discussed how the B-A-C-H motto is both connected to and seeks to be connected to the tonic.

The d-minor triad can also be viewed as a pillar of tonal stability between two pitches from outside the pure diatonic. The midpoints of the ground theme (c♯) and the ground-theme inversion (b♭) are members of both the d-harmonic and d-melodic minor scales. It is significant that these two pitches require written accidentals in order to notationally represent their respective [black key] half-step relationships to the root and fifth of the d-minor triad (Ex. 16).

EXAMPLE 16

These half-step relationships are emphasized in both the ground theme and its inversion (Ex. 17). The melodic line of the ground theme opens with an ascending perfect-fifth leap (d to a), followed by an immediate change in direction. The tonic triad is then filled in as the line passes downward through f on its return to the tonic pitch. Directly after the tonic triad, the pitch c♯ enters. This c♯ functions as the leading tone of the following tonic (d). The inverted form of the ground theme also begins with a tonic triad [starting and ending on the fifth], but this time it is the half step b♭-a that directly follows.

EXAMPLE 17

---

[7] [Translator's note: This concept of pitch-system symmetry is a further possible reference to *Sein;* that is, God as "Alpha and Omega."]

In addition, these half-step bordering pitches also have other important implications for the entire cycle, especially in regard to: 1) the generation of the pitches B-A-C-H; 2) the development of expressive content in the ground theme; and 3) the formation of the total harmonic structure.

B-A-C-H

As we discussed in chapter 1, the discant clausula (c#-d) is found in the ground theme, whereas the pathopoetic motive (a-bb-a) appears only in the inversion of the ground theme. We have also discussed how the entire B-A-C-H-C#-D theme can be derived from these two half-step motives. For that reason, the B-A-C-H-C#-D theme can be considered a thematic projection that originates at the midpoint of the ground theme. Furthermore, the pitches c#-d are frequently associated with the pitch group bb -a-c-b♮. In this study, we shall call this group of six variously ordered pitches the *B-A-C-H sphere*.[8] These tones appear together a number of times during the course of the work and prepare the ear for the entry of the maturely formed B-A-C-H-C#-D theme (the third subject of the closing fugue).

Bach's choice of key was indeed fortuitous. The key of d minor creates a pitch framework which makes it possible to unite the B-A-C-H motto with the discant clausula. To some extent, the ground theme itself shares in this same unification process, since it is also a strong melodic/thematic representation of d minor. Those musical elements of the ground theme which prefigure this unification are particularly noticeable in the tonal answer [to be discussed later, see Ex. 23] and its inversion [Ex. 24]. These elements provide direct evidence that the composer conceived the B-A-C-H-C#-D theme at the very beginning stages of his work on *The Art of Fugue*. Moreover, the presence of these elements also support our view that the B-A-C-H-C#-D theme is a symbol which unlocks the hidden meaning of this work.

It appears that Bach planned both choice of key and the properties of the ground theme in advance so that they would conform to his global conception of the work. This is confirmed in those spots where both the B-A-C-H sphere and the key of d minor are simultaneously stressed. At this point, it may be helpful to examine a few examples which contain the pitches of the B-A-C-H sphere. As might be expected, some occurrences of this pitch group will seem more intentional than others.

In Contrapunctus VI, the countervoice (measure 4, soprano), that follows the initial entry of the subject in the soprano, provides a strong connection

---

[8] [Translator's note: Though the set of six pitches which comprise the B-A-C-H sphere occurs frequently in *The Art of Fugue*, the order of the pitches within the set is not fixed. This makes it possible for the actual B-A-C-H-C#-D theme to emerge gradually from antecedent materials.]

between the key of d minor and the ground theme (Ex. 18). The pitches b♭-a (measure 4) are reminiscent of the pathopoetic b♭-a, which appeared an octave higher in the previous measure, at the midpoint of the subject.[9] Further, this second b♭-a motive is accompanied by the discant-clausula motive (c♯-d) which appears at the midpoint of the alto's entry.[10]

EXAMPLE 18

Beginning of Contrapunctus VI

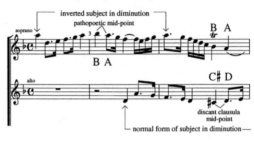

It is difficult to tell whether the B-A-C-H sphere, which appears immediately before the final subject entrance in Contrapunctus V, is intentional. Here, scrambled B-A-C-H pitches in the bass voice are contrapuntally connected to the emphatically repeated discant clausula motive in the soprano (Ex. 19).

EXAMPLE 19

Contrapunctus V

---

[9] [Translator's note: The subject (beginning in measure 2, soprano) appears in both inversion and diminution as compared with the initial subject entry (measure 1, bass).]

The B-A-C-H sphere is also present in the first episode of Contrapunctus I (Ex. 20). Its appearance in this spot also seems somewhat coincidental because the pitches of the group are alternated between the soprano and tenor.[11] Nevertheless, the half-step motives b♭-a (soprano) and c-b♮ (tenor) are stressed in measures 17-18, while the bass winds its way chromatically through the pitches of the B-A-C-H sphere in measures 19-20.

EXAMPLE 20

First Episode of Contrapunctus I

The B-A-C-H sphere present at the end of Contrapunctus IV is probably not coincidental, however (Ex. 21). The pathopoetic motive b♭-a, in the alto [inverted form of the subject], is directly repeated in the tenor. The tenor statement of the motive is then immediately followed by the pitches c-b♮. This yields a completely intact statement of the B-A-C-H motto (measures 135-36, tenor), while the c♯-d figure is emphatically repeated in the soprano. However, the repetition of the discant clausula motive is interrupted in measure 136 by a surprising diminished-fifth leap (e♭-a).[12]

---

[10] [Translator's note: This subject (measure 3, alto) is not inverted like the soprano entry, but does appear in diminution as compared with the initial entry of the subject (measure 1, bass). The soprano entrance (inversion) and the alto entrance (normal form) appear here in stretto.]

[11] Since the alto voice rests during this episode, the tenor voice appears directly below the soprano in Ex. 20.

[12] The interval of a diminished fifth [six half steps] is one half-step smaller than a perfect fifth [seven half steps]. Though its employment prefigures later occurrences, it is only peripheral to our discussion here. It does, however, share some common expressive ground with other materials found in *The Art of Fugue*. Ex. 21 also contains a second diminished fifth (g-c♯, soprano), a diminished fourth (f♯-b♭, tenor) and a rhythmically syncopated half step (b♮-b♭, tenor) inside of the chromatic progression c-b♮-b♭-a. The use of diminished intervals and chromatic motion in *The Art of Fugue* has approximately the same rhetorical meaning that we have attributed to the pitches of the B-A-C-H sphere.

EXAMPLE 21

End of Contrapunctus IV

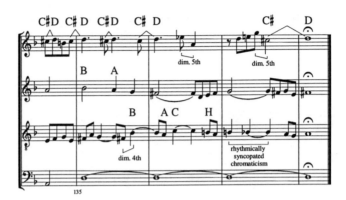

It is necessary to point out that Contrapunctus IV is not found in the Berlin Autograph.[13] This fugue is only introduced in the first printed edition of *The Art of Fugue,* where it appears as the last movement in the group of four simple fugues.[14] An analogy can be drawn between the pitches b-a-c-h-c♯-d at the end of Contrapunctus IV (the last of the four simple fugues) and the B-A-C-H-C♯-D theme (the last of the "new" subjects) in the closing fugue.

We can even take this analogy a step further, if we consider the possibility that alpha-numeric symbolism was deliberately fashioned into the revised coda of Contrapunctus I.[15]

---

[13] [Translator's note: The Berlin Autograph is a volume of forty folio pages, bound in upright format, which contains fair copies of the early drafts to most of the movements. This manuscript is in Bach's own hand. It is called the Berlin Autograph because it is housed as "Mus. ms. autogr. Bach P200" in the Deutsche Staatsbibliothek, Berlin. The index to Bach's works *(Bach Werke Verzeichnis)* lists the contents of this bound volume as BWV 1080:1-3; 5-10a; 11-15. In addition, there are another eleven loose pages of folio that accompany this bound manuscript (BWV 1080:14;18;19). The author describes the contents of the bound pages, but not the loose pages in Table 1, p. 109. For a full description of the Berlin Autograph, see Hans Gunter Hoke, *Zu Johann Sebastian Bachs 'Die Kunst der Fuge'* (1974), a supplemental study to Johann Sebastian Bach, *Die Kunst der Fuge, Autograph, Originaldruck* (Leipzig: VEB Deutscher Verlag für Musik, 1979.)]

[14] [Translator's note: Contrapuncti I-IV. The term "simple fugue" refers to a fugue which contains only a single subject.]

[15] In the first printed version of the work, measures 73-4 of Contrapunctus I are altered, as compared to the contents of the Berlin Autograph. Measures 75-8 of the printed edition were apparently newly composed and included in the movement sometime after the appearance of the Berlin Autograph.

Bach probably changed the original ending of Contrapunctus I in order to increase the sense of musical drama at the close of the fugue. The revised coda presents one more entry of the subject (tenor) above a tonic pedal point. In addition, the accompanying soprano voice in this passage (Ex. 22) ascends, full of expression, before it suddenly leaps downward by diminished seventh (bb-c#) into the final cadence. It may or may not be a coincidence that this soprano-voice passage contains exactly fourteen pitches. Returning to our analogy, it is not impossible that Bach could have invented both a new coda to Contrapunctus I and a completely new movement (Contrapunctus IV) in order to make the B-A-C-H idea more prominent.

EXAMPLE 22

End of Contrapunctus I

Thematic Expression in the Ground Theme

In chapter 1, we discussed how the midpoint of the ground theme (d-c#-d) and the midpoint of the ground-theme inversion (a-bb-a) initiate two separate and opposing areas of musical expression, and how both these expressive gestures initiate the materials of the B-A-C-H-C#-D theme. The discant clausula figure (c#-d) is a gesture of consummation, of tension coming to rest, while the pathopoetic half-step figure (bb-a) characterizes struggle, suffering, and unrest. This basic two-pole assertion, which we have described with the terms *Sein* and *Dasein,* is therefore already present in germ form at the center of the ground theme (d-c#-d).[16]

There are three important melodic variants of the ground theme—its tonal answer, its inversion, and the inversion's tonal answer. The expressive characteristics of these variants warrant closer inspection, since their musical materials are so intimately related to the original ground theme. In fact, these thematic variants appear almost as often as the ground theme itself.

---

[16] [Translator's note: Both the pathopoetic half-step motive (d-c#) and the discant clausula (c#-d) are present in the returning-tone figure (d-c#-d), found at the mid-point of the ground theme.]

The ground theme's tonal answer (Ex. 23) appears in the dominant key (a-minor).[17] In Contrapunctus I, the B-A-C-H sphere can be detected as early as the answer's second half (measures 7-8, soprano).

EXAMPLE 23

The Answer Form of the Ground Theme: Contrapunctus I

The inversion of the ground theme (Ex. 24) reaches the tonic pitch through a downward perfect-fifth leap (a-d). The rest of the tonic triad is then filled out in the opposite direction (f-a). After the pitches of the d-minor triad have been stated, the line then moves directly into the stressed pathopoetic motive (bb-a).[18]

EXAMPLE 24

The Inverted Form of the Ground Theme: Contrapunctus III

It has been suggested that Bach actually based the ground theme of *The Art of Fugue* on Martin Luther's chorale *Aus tiefer Not schrei ich zu dir* (In deep distress I cry unto Thee). Indeed, there is great similarity between the first phrase of this chorale tune and the ground-theme inversion. Like the chorale tune itself, the opening and ending choruses of Cantata 38 *(Aus tiefer Not schrei ich zu dir)* and the organ chorale on the same title (BWV 686) are set in E-Phrygian mode.[19]

---

[17] [Translator's note: The subject is usually stated in the tonic key by the first entering voice at the beginning of a fugue. The next entering voice, however, states the same basic melodic materials transposed into the dominant key. This dominant-key entry is called the answer. The first section (exposition) of a fugue is usually constructed by alternating the subject and the answer until all the voices have entered. When the answer is an exact transposition of the subject into the key of the dominant, it is called a *real answer*. In certain fugues, however, the key connection between the alternating subject and answer must be made less abrupt. In such cases, a few of the intervals in the answer are slightly altered from those found in the subject. When an answer is not an interval-for-interval transposition of the subject, it is known as a *tonal answer*. Since the ground theme's answer is not an exact transposition of the subject, it is considered a tonal answer.]

[18] The first two pitches of the B-A-C-H motto.

[19] Phrygian mode is a diatonic scale with half steps (in the ascending direction) between the first and second, and fifth and sixth scale degrees. The E-Phrygian mode is formed if a stepwise one-octave segment is played on the white notes of the keyboard starting from the pitch E.

In the cantata and the organ chorale, however, Bach employs a two-note motive in the melody where the word *schrei* (cry out) appears, even though this motive is not actually found in the original chorale tune (Ex. 25).[20]

EXAMPLE 25

first phrase of the chorale-tune "Aus tiefer Not" (transposed to D-minor)

pathopoetic returning-tone figure

A   B♭   A   original chorale-tune note

Aus   tie - fer   Not   schrei   ich   zu   dir
[In   deep   dis - stress   cry   I   to   Thee]

Contrapunctus III Ground Theme (inverted form)

Bach's inserted two-note motive

alto   6

A   B♭   A

pathopoetic returning-tone figure

Of all Luther's chorale melodies, *Aus tiefer Not* was the best known by Bach, and certainly the composer would have been conscious of the similarity between the first phrase of this tune and the inversion of the ground theme. The large number of contrapuntal possibilities contained in the ground theme make its derivation from this chorale melody very unlikely, however. Furthermore, if the ground theme had actually been derived from the chorale, its inversion would have probably exchanged places with its normal form at the beginning of *The Art of Fugue*.

A comparison between the two melodies is, nevertheless, quite revealing. The text of the chorale tune, at the point where the pitches a-b♭-a are employed ("deep distress cry"), provides us with evidence that the pathopoetic returning-tone figure (a-b♭-a) found in the inverted ground theme could indeed be symbolic of the "human condition." Bach might have even borrowed this same returning-tone figure and used it in *The Art of Fugue* because of its textual association with the distress of the "human condition."

Although the tonal answer of the inverted ground theme begins and ends with the tonic, it is the most distantly related of the three variants to the original ground theme (Ex. 26).

---

[20] [Translator's note: A line containing the inverted ground theme has been added by the translator to the author's example in Ex. 25 so that the similarity between the inverted ground theme and the chorale tune can be more immediately obvious.]

EXAMPLE 26

The Tonal Answer of the Inverted Ground Theme: Contrapunctus III

A special feature of the inverted answer is an ascending a-minor triad which directly follows a downward perfect-fourth leap. The fifth (e) of this triad is one step higher than the opening pitch d, and it is at this point, after the line crosses above the tonic, that the pathopoetic returning-tone figure enters. Further, this returning-tone figure (e-f-e) is particularly prominent at the line's melodic climax.

A second important feature is the altered quasi-symmetry of its structure. The third pitch (c♮) is changed to c♯ at its corresponding point of symmetry in the second half of the line. This change was necessary for tonal reasons; that is, it was necessary to change the third of the a-minor triad (c♮) into the leading tone of d minor (c♯) so that the line could smoothly return to the key of d minor [in preparation for the following subject entry in the tonic]. Chromatic alteration of the same scale degree in the answer of a non-modulating subject is quite rare in the fugues of Bach, however.

Contrary to the standard rules of fugue, Bach begins Contrapunctus III with the answer form of the inverted subject rather than the subject form. Further, after introducing the c♯ (measure 4, tenor) the line returns chromatically again to c♮ at the beginning of the countersubject (measure 5, tenor). Thus, even as early as Contrapunctus III, the entire work is led into the realm of chromatic expression through the alteration of this single thematic pitch.[21] It should also be mentioned again that the pathopoetic returning-tone figure (e-f-e) is given special prominence in the answer form of the inverted ground theme.

The Harmonic Impulse

We shall now return once more to the pitch c♯, which serves as the central axis of the ground theme. This tone not only originates melodic chromaticism, but it also initiates basic harmonic progression in the work.

---

[21] This launching of chromatic materials will be further discussed in chapter 7, p.69.

Example 27 shows the fundamental harmonic framework of *The Art of Fugue*. As we discussed above, the opposing pitches c♯ and b♭ are extracted from the midpoints of the normal and inverted forms of the ground theme. In Example 27, these two pitches provide the upper and lower half-step border to both the perfect fifth (d-a) and the complete d-minor tonic triad. A complete diminished-seventh chord, distinguished by its lack of a sounding root, harmonic instability, and need for resolution is formed when the interval between the c♯ and b♭ is filled in with [diatonic] thirds. Both sides of our interpretation (*Sein* and *Dasein*) are supported by this simple harmonic progression. The consonant sphere, represented by the tonic triad, is the embodiment of completeness and symbolic of *Sein;* the dissonant sphere, represented by the diminished-seventh chord, is the embodiment of incompleteness, thus symbolic of *Dasein.* Furthermore, this diminished-seventh chord both moves away from and progresses towards the tonic triad.

EXAMPLE 27

Fundamental Harmonic Progression in *The Art of Fugue*

The fundamental harmonic progression shown in Example 27 is encountered as early as the exposition of Contrapunctus I. In this opening fugue, every appearance of the central pitch c♯ (or g♯ in the answer) is as a member of a diminished-seventh chord. In measure 11 of Contrapunctus I (Ex. 28), the midpoint of the subject (c♯) sounds in the bass while the tenor sounds the pitch g. At the same time, the soprano voice moves in eighth notes from b♭ to e. This treatment of the diminished-seventh chord is typical of Bach.

The diminished-seventh chord (circled in Ex. 28) consists of two interlocking diminished fifths (c♯-g; b♭-e). In the Baroque era, the diminished fifth was thought to be a "false" or "deficient" fifth, since it lacks the stability of the perfect fifth. Therefore, in our interpretation, the "false" fifth will also represent aspects of the "human condition." Looking further at the soprano line in Example 28, one may or may not find it a coincidence that the false fifth (b♭-e) interrupts an otherwise smooth linear connection between the pitches b♭-a [B-A] and c-b♮ [C-H].

EXAMPLE 28

The exposition of Contrapunctus I: Middle of the Third Entry

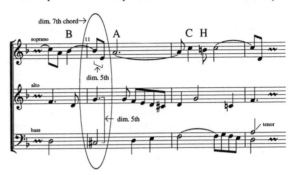

The Motion Impulse

The pitch c♯ is not only the generator of chromatic space and its associated harmonic processes, but it also provides an impetus for forward rhythmic motion in the ground theme.

As Example 29 shows, the central c♯ assumes the role of the leading tone, which tends to propel the melodic line forward. Because this c♯ is located on the downbeat of the measure, a balancing rhythmic motion in quarter notes carries the line forward, away from the leading tone, through the tonic (d) and into the tied half note (f), which falls on the downbeat of the following measure. This tied half note should be considered more than just one of the poles in the thematic symmetry. Reached by way of the half-step motion (e-f), it is not only the goal of the preceding quarter-note motion, but it also exhibits a "false-fourth" [diminished-fourth] relationship to the central c♯. Because of this false-fourth relationship, the f seems relatively unstable despite (or perhaps, because of) its proportionally longer duration. The tied-note figure then produces a further rhythmic impetus for the eighth-note passage which follows.

The five pitches at the end of the ground theme provide the most important source of motion in the entire work, a rhythmic impetus which is prepared in two separate ways.

EXAMPLE 29

Rhythmic impetus in the Ground Theme

1) The last four notes of the ground theme, whose pitches are contained within a perfect fourth, are consistently employed as an *anacrusis*[22] at the beginning of the countervoices, countersubjects, and episodes.[23] Whether this figure is extracted from the normal form of the ground theme or whether it comes from the ground-theme inversion, or one of the other ground-theme variants, we shall refer to it as the *thematic eighth-note figure.* This rhythmic figure generates a characteristic motion that can be traced through an entire movement, whether the figure and its variants are linked together in a chain, or connected to other motives. The presence of the thematic eighth-note figure represents the ground theme wherever it appears in the entire work.

We shall now examine some arbitrary spots in the score where thematic eighth-note figures appear. Perhaps it will be sufficient here, as in other places in this study, to cite only a few examples. Starting with the eighth-note motive from the end of the ground theme or one of its variants (⌐), Example 30 illustrates several methods by which the thematic eighth-note figure can be linked to itself and continued forward.

EXAMPLE 30

Variations of the thematic eight-note figure in *The Art of Fugue*

a) Contrapunctus II

b) Contrapunctus IV

c) Contrapunctus VI

d) Contrapunctus VI

e) Contrapunctus XI

f) Contrapunctus XIIa

---

[22] An *anacrusis* is a metrically unstressed single tone (upbeat; pickup) or a group of metrically unstressed tones which begin a musical phrase.

2) The thematic eighth-note figure can also be pushed forward melodically by means of contrapuntal pressure from another voice. In Example 31, the alto voice moves into a perfect-fourth dissonance against the tied-over soprano (c). This dissonance creates a contrapuntal pressure on the tied-over note which pushes the line forward in eighth notes toward resolution. Hereafter, we shall refer to this kind of two-voice harmonic pressure as a *contrapuntal nudge*.[24] Leafing through the score, one can observe many spots where this device is employed. As Example 31 shows, the contrapuntal nudge even appears in the early measures of Contrapunctus I.

EXAMPLE 31

The Contrapuntal-Nudge Figure: Contrapunctus I

We can only complete our investigation of how the ground theme provides unity for the entire work after further examination of its potential for variation and the ways Bach utilizes that potential. It is also important that we study the progressive formal symmetry of the ground theme and how it is projected into the overall form of *The Art of Fugue*. In all of this, however, we must not only apply our findings to the analysis of musical materials and compositional techniques, but also to our interpretation. We should have a better understanding of the fundamental importance of the ground theme after we examine the topics of variation, structure, and order in the cycle (chapters 8 and 9).

---

[23] [Translator's note: Whereas a countersubject (in its technical definition) is a regularly recurring voice which accompanies the subject, a counter voice is a "free" accompanimental voice which does not regularly recur. Episodes are those sections of a fugue where the subject (or answer) is not present.]

[24] In chapter 6, it will be shown that the contrapuntal nudge does not always require a dissonant impetus.

6

Contrapunctus

T he terms "fugue," "canon," and "contrapunctus" are all used as titles in *The Art of Fugue*. Whereas the term "fugue" appears only in the title of the entire work, Bach included four movements which he entitled "canons," while each bonafide fugue is called a "contrapunctus." We shall now discuss the questions surrounding the use of these terms and their implied meanings.

Johannes Mattheson provides us with a description of fugue as it was understood in the time of Bach.[1] He writes that "each voice takes flight, one before the other, and this flight pleasantly continues until the voices finally come together and are reconciled with one another."[2]

The term "canon," as it was used in the Baroque, actually had nearly the same meaning as fugue. Johann Gottfried Walther defined the canon as a "type of fugue;" that is, a "strict or bound fugue" (*Fuga ligata*), whereas the fugue [as we understand it today] was called "free or specific fugue" (*Fuga libera oder particularis*).[3] Because of the similar meanings of the terms "canon" and "fugue," *The Art of Fugue* is an appropriate title, despite Bach's inclusion of canons in the work. However, the title, *The Art of Fugue*, does not appear on the autograph manuscripts in Bach's own hand.

---

[1] See: Johannes Mattheson, *Der Vollkommene Capellmeister* (1739) contained in *Documenta Musicologia*, erste Reihe, Nr. 5; also published by the same title in a modern edition by Margaret Reimann (Kassel: Bärenreiter-Verlag, 1954).

[2] The Latin term *fuga* means flight.

[3] Johann Gottfried Walther, *Musikalisches Lexikon oder Musikalische Bibliothek*, 1732. This treatise is available in facsimile, ed. Richard Schall (Kassel: Bärenreiter-Verlag, 1953). For additional information on various types of canon and canonic procedures see also the chapter entitled "Von der Fuga Totali" in Johann Gottfried Walther, *Præcepta der musicalischen Composition* (1708); modern edition by Peter Benary (Leipzig: Breitkopf und Härtel Musikverlag, 1955).

Die Kunst der Fuge [*The Art of Fugue*], written on the first page of the Berlin Autograph, was inscribed by Bach's son-in-law, Johann Christoph Altnikol. This same title, but in the form *Kunst der Fuga*, appears on the covers of the two folders containing supplemental pages to the Berlin Autograph.[4] These titles are in the hand of Bach's second youngest son, Johann Christoph Friedrich Bach. Perhaps the composer was himself undecided about the title of the work, and though the title *Kunst der Fuga* is a possibility, he could have just as easily named the work *Kunst des Contrapuncts* or *Ars contrapuncti* (The Art of Counterpoint).

A question remains—why is the title "contrapunctus" used with the fugues, but not the canons? If we assume that Bach intended to call the closing fugue a contrapunctus, the entire work would then contain fourteen contrapuncti [fugues]. This number brings to mind again the possibility of symbolic intention. Moreover, the idea that the complete work is constructed from fourteen contrapuncti certainly corresponds with the meaning of the B-A-C-H motto as we have interpreted it. The presence of these fourteen fugues is also additional evidence in favor of the statement: "I, Bach, have composed this work"; and further, "I [Bach] identify myself with this work and its message." However, if Bach actually intended this symbolic self-reference, it would appear that only the fugues (contrapuncti) were intended to take part in it.

Why should the canons be excluded? Though Bach could have differentiated between contrapuncti and canons on the basis of number symbolism, such a hypothesis is neither provable nor even completely plausible. It is possible, however, that Bach might have considered the fugue the better of the two media for purposes of demonstrating his contrapuntal craft. Although the canons in *The Art of Fugue* are no less artistically conceived, during the Baroque, canon was valued primarily as a paragon of strict contrapuntal procedure *(Fuga ligata)*, whereas the fugue *(Fuga libera oder particularis)* was thought to be a better medium for free contrapuntal expression.

Counterpoint is a technical procedure of composition, whereas fugue (including canon) is a musical form. The title of the work directly connects compositional technique *(The Art of)* to a form *(Fugue)*. If we assume that *The Art of Fugue* was the title Bach intended for the work, it is clear that his purpose was to demonstrate contrapuntal craft by means of fugue.

During Bach's time, counterpoint was not yet firmly attached to specific musical genres. According to Walther, "Every harmonic relationship is actually counterpoint."[5] Though this comprehensive statement about contrapuntal expression comes from the time of Bach, its origins can actually be traced back

---

[4] BWV 1080:14;18;19.

[5] Walther, *Musikalisches Lexikon oder Musikalische Bibliothek*, 1732.

to the late Middle Ages. In fact, this broad concept of counterpoint has been synonymous with established norms of musical composition since early modern times. Walther also states that "counterpoint is a term that was formerly applied to composition itself,"[6] and he further defines composition as "the science of setting consonance and dissonance together in such a way that they purify each other and establish harmony."[7]

It was only during the time of Bach that composers began to conceive works independently from counterpoint. In the eighteenth century, a new concept of composition gradually replaced the long-standing ideal of counterpoint as composition; that is, contrapuntal considerations became less important in the process of determining musical materials and texture [than, for instance, aspects of functional harmony]. It was also during this time that counterpoint came to be associated with specific musical forms.

A contrapunctus is defined as: 1) a subject-based composition;[8] 2) a composition in which the individual voices may appear in various positions relative to one another (contrapuntal devices ranging from simple non-invertible counterpoint to more complex double-, triple-, and even quadruple-, etc.; invertible counterpoint may be employed in a contrapunctus); and 3) a basic note-against-note texture (*punctus contra punctum*), meaning that the structure of musical intervals in a contrapunctus depends upon numerical relationships (*numeri*) and mathematical proportions (*proportiones, rationes*). Walther wrote, "the bringing together of sounding voices" is "a mathematical science. . . . Music generally borrows its [technical] interrelationships from the field of mathematics, most notably from the fields of geometry and arithmetic, where proportions and numbers (*proportiones et numeri*) are particularly important."[9]

During the time of Bach, however, the tradition of contrapunctus-based compositions was already regarded as old-fashioned. As employed by Bach's contemporaries, the term "contrapunctus" implied a specific method of composing that was usually associated with works from the past. Roman Catholic composers placed special importance on contrapunctus during the Baroque, since counterpoint embodied a continuation or re-experiencing of the musical

---

[6] Walther, *Præcepta der musicalischen Composition*, 1708.

[7] Walther, *Musikalisches Lexikon oder Musikalische Bibliothek*, 1732.

[8] The term *subject* here refers to the use of a preexisting melody, such as a cantus, cantus firmus or theme.

[9] Walther, *Præcepta der musicalischen Composition*, 1708.

tradition venerated by the Council of Trent (1543-63).[10] The contrapuntal music of this tradition is highly controlled, strict, pure, and solemn. Thus, Catholic composers tended to closely associate counterpoint with sacred music. This austere tradition is exemplified during the Baroque in the counterpoint text *Gradus ad Parnassum* by Johann Joseph Fux.[11]

Outside of the Catholic Church, however, and especially in Protestant Germany, sacred music in the Baroque had only a minimal connection with the old strict style. Music from the golden age of counterpoint was shunned by the German Protestants, who considered counterpoint an ancient means of musical expression, full of mannered and academic practices. Mattheson claimed that *contrapunct* was actually a "barbaric name" applied to multivoiced composi-tions.[12] Earlier, Mattheson even spoke of that "old, tiresome, and incomprehen-sible *Contra-Punct* style."[13] The caustic remarks of Friedrich Erhard Niedt go even further. For him, counterpoint was "a great musical wonder-animal" of which the musical "sophist, eccentric, and fool" could not get enough. Niedt then went on to say that "it was not worth the trouble to smear paper with this doubled, inverted, salted, larded, fried, and basted with rabbit drippings contrapunct, since it contains absolutely no [musical] affections."[14] Bach was certainly aware of this widespread disdain for counterpoint. Furthermore, he must have had to endure the brunt of many such pointed remarks. Most certainly he was concerned and deeply troubled by the anti-contrapuntal vitriol preached by so many of his contemporaries.

Counterpoint is absolutely fundamental to Bach's musical art. Furthermore, his contrapuntal works are concrete examples of technique grounded in the three principles of contrapunctus described above. The high percentage of subject compositions in the complete works of Bach certainly demonstrates that he relied heavily on techniques of the old polyphonic school. Moreover, Bach's subject-

---

[10] [Translator's note: The Council of Trent nearly abolished all music in the Church other than plainsong, because of problems associated with text clarity and the increasing secularization of multi-voice works that had taken place over the years. As a result of the influence of Jacobus de Kerle and others (including Palestrina), the Cardinals were convinced that the more solemn and austere polyphonic styles should be allowed to continue in the Mass.]

[11] [Translator's note: Johann Joseph Fux, *Gradus ad Parnassum*, (Vienna, 1725). According to Fux, this text presents the principles of strict counterpoint modeled on the pure vocal polyphony of Palestrina (1525-94). Fux also adds a number of more modern contrapuntal devices and techniques, however.]

[12] Mattheson, *Der Vollkommene Capellmeister*, 1739.

[13] [Translator's note: Mattheson prepared a prepublication draft (*Vorabdruck*) in Weimar of the later appearing *Musik Lexicon* (1732). This was published by D. Limplecht (Erfurt, 1728).]

[14] Friedrich Erhardt Niedt, *Musicalsiche Handleitung* (Hamburg,1717).

based compositions presuppose that the musical materials will be capable of contrapuntal manipulation.

It is also clear that proportional interrelationships are vital organizational principles in Bach's polyphonic music. At the same time, however, his works, and especially the subject-based pieces, show a compositional mastery that went far beyond mere adoption of old-school models. In terms of technique and expression, Bach continually explored and pushed ahead into new musical territory; this is especially true in *The Art of Fugue*.

Bach left no record of why he composed *The Art of Fugue*, but it stands to reason that he thought of this work both as a demonstration of his compositional prowess, and as a defense of contrapuntal art against those who would bring it into disrepute. It is as if he is using this work as a vehicle to say: "now I shall show you what contrapunctus is and what I understand it to be."

The Art of Fugue and Mizler's Society for the Study of Music

Hans Gunter Hoke strongly argues that Bach intended *The Art of Fugue* to be a musical essay in defense of counterpoint. This thesis is presented during a discussion about Bach's role in the *Societät der musikalischen Wissenschaften* (Society for the Study of Music).[15] This association, dating from the year 1738, was founded in Leipzig by Lorenz Christoph Mizler, who was a university lecturer in mathematics, physics, and music, and a former student of Bach. Bach was admitted as its fourteenth member in June of 1747. The bylaws of the society required that every member submit "at least one treatise per year" until the member's sixty-fifth birthday.[16] These bylaws further stipulated that, "every member should, at every opportunity, strive to speak and write against the misuse of music and against those hacks and scorners who seek to abolish [contrapuntal] church music, to the end that a better appraisal of traditional practices might be established, that the majesty of old music might be better appreciated, and that the genre itself might be improved and its passions refined."

Bach submitted his six-voice canonic variations on the Christmas chorale *Von Himmel hoch, da komm' ich her* to Mizler's Society for his initiation in 1747. This submission fulfilled Bach's obligation for that year; his obligation for 1748 was probably fulfilled in the autumn of 1747 with the printed score of *The Musical Offering*. In 1749, the last year he was required to make a submission, it is quite possible that he wished to submit *The Art of Fugue*. If true, this could

---

[15] Hans Gunter Hoke, *Zu Johann Sebastian Bachs 'Die Kunst der Fuge'* (1974), a supplemental study to: Johann Sebastian Bach, *Die Kunst der Fuge,* Autograph, Originaldruck (Leipzig: VEB Deutscher Verlag für Musik, 1979).

[16] Musical compositions could be submitted in lieu of a treatise.

explain his hurry to engrave the completed fugues even before the composition of the entire work was finished. Nevertheless, we should not conclude that Bach's primary reason for composing *The Art of Fugue* was the fulfillment of his obligation to Mizler's Society. On the basis of handwriting analysis and an examination of the paper used in the autograph, Christoph Wolff has shown that Bach could have started working on the fair copy [Berlin Autograph] as early as 1740.[17]

The question of the work's date of origin and its connection with Mizler's Society requires no further discussion here. There is no doubt that Bach was involved in the defense of counterpoint against widespread contemporary scorn and that he found support for his views and musical activities in Mizler's Society. It is difficult to believe, however, that Bach composed *The Art of Fugue* simply so "that the majesty of old music might be better appreciated." *The Art of Fugue* was not conceived as old music, but rather as new music based on a strong and proven foundation. In short, this composition demonstrates the art of counterpoint as Bach understood it.

Counterpoint is absolutely essential to Bach's style. In fact, it was so important to him that he took pains to design his polyphonic works so that they would not contradict the new harmonic principles evolving at that time. Furthermore, one need only glance at the other music of this era to discover that Bach's compositions far surpass those of his contemporaries in terms of rhetorical content, musical affection, and dramatic expression.

The Gradual Development of Complexity in *The Art of Fugue*

The Art of Fugue demonstrates Bach's compositional processes in a particularly appropriate form. According to Mattheson, "a fugue, like all multivoice forms, is a contrapunctus, but not all contrapuncti are fugues."[18] This implies that certain technical devices are required for the realization of a fugue. Among these are multiple-invertible counterpoint, melodic and rhythmic imitation, inversion, augmentation, diminution, retrograde, and retrograde inversion.

It is not difficult to see a similarity between the way that musical materials and techniques are developed within an individual fugue and the process by which each succeeding movement in *The Art of Fugue* presents an ever-increasing level of contrapuntal complexity. It also appears that Bach employed recurring musical materials in order to demonstrate that counterpoint can powerfully maintain both musical unity and variety. Unity is firmly established

---

[17] Christoph Wolff, "Zur Chronologie und Kompositionsgeschichte von Bachs 'Kunst der Fuge'," in *Beitrag zur Musikwissenschaft* (1983): 130-142.

[18] Mattheson, *Der Vollkommene Capellmeister*, 1739.

in *The Art of Fugue* by the use of subjects [and subject-based materials] that are directly related to the ground theme, whereas the diverse character of the fugues and their ever-increasing complexity provide elements of variety. Even the definition of the term "contrapunctus," which appears as the title for each fugal movement, implies [according to Mattheson] a sense of technical variety.

Nevertheless, Bach's idea of limiting musical materials to those derived from a single subject has a restraining influence on technical development in *The Art of Fugue*. By limiting the movements of the work to a single form (fugue), and by further limiting all movements to musical materials derived from a single subject, Bach greatly restricted his possibilities of compositional choice. The challenge was to invent a ground theme which contained enough latent possibilities of variation and expression that each fugue in the cycle would appear fresh and exciting; this despite the fact that all the subjects were to be derived from the same theme and that the musical form [fugue] would remain constant throughout.

The fugue (*fuga libera oder particularis*) is a better vehicle for the demonstration of contrapuntal expression than other types of subject-based compositions; e.g., than chorale arrangements, chorale hymn settings, or aria variations. In this regard, fugue is even superior to canon (*fuga ligata*). This is because fugue consists of two basic textures— one, where the subject (or answer) is present,[19] and the other [episode], where the subject is not present, but where "free" counterpoint is employed. The sheer intensity of episodic counterpoint at the end of *The Art of Fugue* has never been surpassed (more about this later), but even the strict subject-based sections of the work do not lack in expressive character.

A subject acts like a preexisting melody in both the exposition and entry sections of a fugue. Since it enters voice-by-voice according to plan, and since it is then subjected to a number of later developments and modulatory schemes, the subject (in an ideal sense) behaves like a wandering cantus firmus, appearing sometimes here, sometimes there. Indeed, the subject is truly a cantus firmus in the sense that it was developed and committed to paper before the rest of the fugue was composed.

The structure of a fugue exhibits the following basic properties: 1) *connection to the theme*—all musical activity in a fugue proceeds from a single source; that is, each voice of a fugue is initiated by and carried forward from a statement of the subject; 2) *equality of voices*—all voices in a fugue are equal carriers of the theme; 3) *linear quality*—due to equality of the voices, the polyphonic, independent character of each voice is imprinted with and characterized by the

---

[19] [Translator's note: The subject and answer are imitatively introduced and knitted together in the exposition section of the work. After the exposition is completed, however, further appearances of the subject or answer in the body of a fugue are called entries.]

subject; and 4) *cantus firmus like attributes*—the theme provides a preexisting succession of points and lines that can be set against opposing points and lines.

These same four structural principles can also be specifically applied to countervoices. The contrapuntal relationship between the subject and a countervoice establishes a musical connection to the subject. Moreover, because of its contrapuntal relationship to the subject, a countervoice maintains both equality of voice and its own linear character. A countervoice can also possess the attributes of a cantus firmus, especially when it is employed as a regularly recurring countersubject.

In *The Art of Fugue*, the countervoices are structurally related to and expressively motivated by the subject; that is, the countervoices incorporate and develop particular musical gestures and expressive ideas which are found in the subject. At least until episodic materials enter, the countervoices often raise a particular thematic gesture from a position of local importance to one that becomes significant for an entire movement. In short, every contrapunctus in *The Art of Fugue* is a reflection of the musical materials found in its subject.

Example 32 contains the first eleven measures of Contrapunctus I. This excerpt demonstrates the cohesive character of the musical materials in *The Art of Fugue*.

EXAMPLE 32

The beginning of Contrapunctus I

In the first measure of Contrapunctus I, the alto states the ground theme in its subject form, but the actual compositional process does not begin until the entry of the tonal answer (measure 5, soprano). Note that the answer enters at the same time as the last tone of the subject. This elision of subject and answer is actually a double elision, since the last note of the subject (alto) also becomes the first note of the countervoice.

The stepwise ascending quarter notes, which move from the tonic to the dominant at the beginning of the countervoice, can be viewed as a melodic filling in of the perfect-fifth leap which opened the subject. This passage can also be regarded as a stepwise ascending continuation of the pitch succession (d-e-f) away from the subject's central c♯. The beginning of the countervoice (d-e-f-g) can even be considered an inversion of the subject's last four pitches (g-f-e-d). In addition, the rhythmically strong harmonic intervals (*punctus contra punctum*) found between the start of the answer and the beginning of the countervoice (perfect fifth; major sixth; minor third) are further emphasized by this quarter-note motion.

The inconspicuous downward leap of an octave (measure 6, alto) is the very first example in *The Art of Fugue* of the contrapuntal principle that a voice may freely leap to other notes of the same chordal sonority (here the leap takes place within the a-minor triad). Henceforth, we shall refer to this kind of motion as a *leap within the chord*.

In measure six, the countervoice (alto) proceeds into the quarter note f by means of eighth-note motion. If we examine the local harmonic progression here, this note seems at first somewhat ambiguous and out of place. This f, however, is tied-over in a similar fashion to the half note f which appears near the end of the subject (measure 4). This tie figure takes on a new and important additional role in measure seven; it initiates a contrapuntal nudge. The midpoint of the answer [soprano's half-note g♯] turns the tied f into a dissonant suspension on the first quarter of measure seven. This dissonant f then requires resolution down by step to e [7-6 suspension]. As will be discussed shortly, this contrapuntal nudge actually initiates the basic musical concept that controls the entire first Contrapunctus. (In Ex. 32, those tied [or dotted note] figures which supply contrapuntal nudges are marked with ⌣ and ⌣.)

Between the suspended f and its resolution to e, however, the line leaps both toward and away from the pitch b♮. Although the leap into b♮ describes a diminished fifth, both f and b♮ clearly belong to the same implied chordal sonority [g♯ diminished-seventh chord]. The diminished-seventh chord's role as an impetus of harmonic motion was covered in chapter 5. From this point, we shall refer to an interrupted suspension resolution as a *resolution through a leap*.

To summarize, there are two important contrapuntal devices exhibited by the alto countervoice pitches f-b♮-e in measures 6-7: 1) the tied quarter note f, similar to the tied half note which appears earlier (measure 4, soprano), becomes part of a contrapuntal-nudge figure; and 2) the diminished-seventh chord is implied (in two-voice texture) between the answer's g♯ and the leap within the chord (f-b♮). [Notice, however, that the diminished-seventh chord is incomplete, since there is no d present in the sonority.]

It is clear that Bach was able to greatly extend the scope of his counterpoint by interrupting basic stepwise melodic progressions with intermediate leaps to chord members which belong to the implied background harmony (leap within the chord). This method of contrapuntal extension is both historically important and a hallmark of Bach's style. Moreover, it helps to explain why Bach was so prolific and why his contrapuntal works can be perceived with such clarity.

Certainly, Bach's multiple-voice counterpoint can still be understood traditionally; that is, as the setting of one pitch against another by specific harmonic intervals (*punctus contra punctum*). Even the melodic leap f-b♮ (measure 7, alto) can be regarded as a diminished fifth (*quinta deficiens*). Nevertheless, it appears that Bach was thinking in terms of functional harmony here. As we have seen, the beginning of measure 7 contains a clearly implied (though incomplete) diminished-seventh chord. Bach seems to abandon stepwise motion in the alto voice in order to clarify the underlying harmony and emphasize the fundamental expressive character of the diminished-fifth (a basic generating interval of the diminished-seventh chord).

We have just discussed the dissonant suspension figure in combination with resolution through a leap as one type of contrapuntal nudge. Before continuing with our analysis, I should like to add a few comments about the contrapuntal nudge which is motivated by a simple tied-note figure.

In measure seven (second quarter), the resolution note e is tied over to the first eighth note of the second beat, while the soprano line moves into the quarter note a. The e and the a form a dissonant perfect fourth at the beginning of beat two. This dissonance creates a new contrapuntal nudge, which is then released by the thematic eighth-note figure, while the answer (soprano) ascends in quarter notes (a-b♮). In measure eight, the contrapuntal relationship between the soprano and alto voices is reversed. The soprano's half note c holds through, while the alto moves in quarter notes (e-f♯) into the half note g.

The soprano's tied-over c, and the alto's g now converge (measure 8, beat 2) to form another contrapuntal nudge (a dissonant perfect fourth). The dissonant tension is again released by the thematic eighth-note figure (soprano), while the alto g is tied across the barline into measure 9. This tied g then forms yet another perfect fourth against d at the entry of the subject in the bass (measure 9, downbeat). This time the dissonance is resolved by the alto's quarter-note f♮.

Meanwhile, the soprano (measure 9) leaps in eighth notes from a downward to d (a leap within the chord) and then upward again to the half note d an octave higher. On the second beat of measure 9, the half note e (alto) then converges with the soprano's half note d, forming a dissonant minor seventh. This minor seventh is resolved by the soprano which moves downward into c♯.

From measure nine into the downbeat of measure ten, a two-voice cadence is formed by the convergence of the soprano's c♯-d motion (discant clausula) with the e-d motion in the alto (tenor clausula). The soprano then leaps downward again within the chord (d-a) and then leaps upward to c♮.[20] The tied-over c♮ in the soprano converges with alto's d, but is not dislodged until the half note d enters in the bass on the second beat of measure ten. The soprano again resolves by way of a leap within the chord to b♭, which now converges with the dotted quarter note (f) in the alto, forming another perfect fourth.[21]

The soprano b♭ is once again tied-over the barline where it forms a diminished seventh against the bass c♯ (measure 11, downbeat). This contrapuntal nudge then resolves through another leap within the chord into the dotted half note (a) in the soprano. A complete c♯ diminished-seventh chord actually occurs on the first quarter of measure eleven, if the eighth-note leap within the chord (soprano) is taken into consideration. These two forms of the contrapuntal nudge, the leap within the chord and the simple tied suspension, then continue throughout the remainder of Contrapunctus I.

Although this kind of "slow motion" analysis is tiresome to read, going through the process does actually help sharpen one's aural and visual perception of Bach's compositional methods. Furthermore, this type of microscopic investigation reveals not only how painstakingly Bach considered the choice of every musical detail and how every note can be interpreted on so many levels, but it also reveals the incredible artistry that is in control. Bach's genius will become even more apparent as we study the relationship between the ground theme and its associated counterpoint.

Before leaving the first measures of Contrapunctus I (Ex. 32), several other details should be noted:

1) The rhythmic pattern (♩. ♪) appears only after it has been first introduced by the tied-note figure (♩|♫). The prefiguring and gradual development of musical materials is basic to Bach's contrapuntal technique, and virtually no materials are employed in *The Art of Fugue* which were not previously prepared.

2) Tied-note figures are important throughout Contrapunctus I, and they seem to be especially noticeable when they occur against entries of the subject or the answer. These tied-note figures are particularly prominent when they are played on stringed keyboard instruments, since the natural decay time of the strings seems to emphasize the nudging-forward of a tied note by a converging dissonant pitch.[22]

---

[20] It should be noted that this leap within the chord is the first occurrence of this figure without a dissonant strong beat impetus.

[21] This time the fourth between soprano and alto is consonant since the bass sounds d, forming a six-three sonority (first inversion triad).

[22] Decay time is the time it takes for the sound to die away after the string is set in motion.

3) The entry of the subject in the bass (measure 9, downbeat) does not coincide with the cadence formed by the soprano (discant clausula) and alto (tenor clausula) at the beginning of measure 10. This elision technique helps keep the voices moving smoothly across intermediate articulations in the form.

4) From measure 6 on, eighth-note motion becomes more and more prominent until, after measure 10, the composite rhythm is nearly always moving forward in eighth notes.

5) The pitches of the B-A-C-H sphere are present, even here at the beginning of Contrapunctus I. Although in scrambled order, these pitches are found in close succession in the answer and its following discant clausula (see Ex. 32, measures 7-9, labeled notes in soprano).

As mentioned previously, the contrapuntal action of this fugue is dominated either by dissonant suspensions which resolve through a leap within the chord or by simple tied-note suspensions. This type of suspension counterpoint, derived from the tied-note figure in measure 4, produces the characteristic musical expression of Contrapunctus I. At the same time, this fugue is also a prototype of the most basic kind of contrapuntal motion; that is, the individual voices of Contrapunctus I strictly maintain their own identity while moving in a constant ebb and flow against each other. In spite of the contrapuntal nudge formed by the converging of one voice against another, the individual voices do not become unduly enmeshed or dependent upon one another, but rather proceed in a self-motivated fashion.

Like Contrapunctus I, each of the other fugues in the cycle also exhibits a particular expressive idea which is always derived from the materials of the ground theme or one of its variants. Bach alters or develops these basic materials differently from fugue to fugue, so that each Contrapunctus is perceived to have its own individual expressive character.

Let us now consider the four Contrapuncti which make up the first group of fugues in *The Art of Fugue*. The first two of these fugues (Contrapuncti I and II) are based on the normal form of the ground theme, and the second two (Contrapuncti III and IV) on the inversion of the ground theme.

As is clear from what has been discussed above, the contrapuntal nudge is the main musical idea behind Contrapunctus I. This forward impetus is created by the use of: 1) the suspension resolution connected to a leap within the chord; and 2) the simple tied-note suspension. In Contrapunctus II, the most important new expressive idea is established by the last four pitches of the subject. The rhythm of these four pitches is altered from the original ground theme so that a characteristic pattern of dotted eighth and sixteenth notes is created. Once this dotted-note pattern is established, it is consistently maintained in at least one of the four voices throughout the rest of the fugue (Ex. 30a and Ex. 47). Heightened chromaticism and sharp dissonances are the primary characteristics of Contrapunctus III (Ex. 33 and Ex. 36), while the leap, especially the downward leap of a third, dominates Contrapunctus IV (Ex. 45).

Once again, the premise that Bach was primarily interested in demonstrating the art of counterpoint (contrapunctus) in the medium of fugue is confirmed. He not only uses the standard contrapuntal techniques throughout *The Art of Fugue* (invertible counterpoint, inversion, mirroring, augmentation and diminution), but he also employs musical motives which possess specific rhetorical meanings. Walther discusses a number of such rhetorical devices,[23] particularly those described and handed down by the contrapuntal teachers of the Italian school, and especially those found in the writings of Angelo Berardi.[24] Walther claimed that certain textures, like the contrapuntal *legato, obligato, syncopation* or *saltando* should only be employed when musical "conditions justify their use." For that reason, "syncopated and leaping contrapuntal motives" are best limited to those places in a score where a composer wishes to create a somewhat "stubborn" musical character.

Bach's treatment of the fourteen contrapuncti in *The Art of Fugue* is actually a specieslike study, since each fugue emphasizes specific and individualized contrapuntal techniques. This specieslike plan is not limited to technical matters, however. Bach also seems to have attached specific and intentional rhetorical meanings to each of the fugues in the cycle. The species approach to matters of both technique and expression is especially helpful when considering the work's first group of four fugues.

In light of our interpretation, the first four fugues can be considered preliminary discourses on *Sein* and *Dasein*. Until the very last section, the musical materials of Contrapunctus I seem to proceed out of the ground theme in a relatively straightforward manner.[25] The first Contrapunctus, therefore, can be considered representative of the "Ground of Being" out of which everything proceeds; therefore "it is" (*es ist*). Contrapunctus II, with its ubiquitous dotted-note rhythms and its obstinate phrasing, asserts "I desire [identification with this 'Ground']" (*ich will*), while the chromaticism and dissonance which dominate the materials of Contrapunctus III, declares, "[alas,] I am" (*ich bin*). In its characteristic outpouring of joy, Contrapunctus IV seems to express the thought, "I shall become [identified with this 'Ground']" (*ich werde sein*).

Granted, these interpretations are highly subjective (and one is under no obligation to accept them), but perhaps they will be able to stand up under further scrutiny. I shall return to them repeatedly in an attempt to advance my thesis.

---

[23] Walther, *Musikalisches Lexikon,* 1732.

[24] See Angelo Berardi, *Documenti armonici* (Boulogna,1687). [Translator's note: Berardi (1630-1694) was an Italian music theorist who published a number of treatises on harmony and related topics.]

[25] The final section of Contrapunctus I will be discussed later. See chapter 7, p.92.

7

Compositional Expression

As was stressed in chapter 6, Bach often employed a contrapunctus movement when he wished to add far-reaching expressive content to a work. Though many of Bach's works are characterized by their richly expressive features, nowhere is his art of contrapuntal expression more refined than in *The Art of Fugue*.

It has often been said that this monothematic cycle of fugues has more value for the scholar than for the listener. In fact, it has hardly ever been regarded as anything more than a prestigious and learned diversion from the practical, a famous design in isolation, or perhaps just a "dry" late work. This esoteric reputation has been earned primarily because of the great number and complexity of contrapuntal devices that Bach employed in *The Art of Fugue*. [1] The work only proves to be fleshless and bloodless, however, if we focus too much attention on its technical aspects.

In the hands of Bach, the fugue became much more than an abstract medium for the demonstration of technical facility. Indeed, Bach's fugues are full of living and breathing expression, maintained by an almost inexhaustible supply of subtle musical inflections. *The Art of Fugue* is particularly unique among the works of Bach, because the composer restricted himself not only to fugal form, but also to a single source-theme from which all subsequent thematic material is derived. For this reason, he designed a ground theme that could be contrapuntally combined and expressively varied in a large number of ways. In this chapter we shall explore some aspects of the great expressive variety that is present in *The Art of Fugue*.

---

[1] The contrapuntal techniques of stretto, inversion, augmentation, diminution, invertible counterpoint, retrograde, mirror technique and various combinations of all of these are employed in *The Art of Fugue*.

The Chromatic

Structural chromaticism, with its closely associated active dissonances, is not introduced in the work until Contrapunctus III. This is in contrast to the relatively diatonic textures found in Contrapuncti I and II.

Of the four simple fugues at the beginning of the work, Contrapunctus III is also the first to employ the inversion form of the ground theme. The coupling of thematic inversion with chromatic materials corresponds to the side of our interpretation which deals with "human frailty." We have previously discussed how both the pathopoetic returning-tone figure (a-bb-a) and chromatic motion in general represent the incomplete nature of human existence *(Dasein).*[2]

Contrapunctus III begins with the answer form of the ground-theme inversion. Though starting a fugue in this manner is very unusual, this reversal of subject and answer clearly illustrates Bach's preference for musical expression over arbitrary rules of fugal procedure. Indeed, he always seems to be seeking some new way of introducing his musical materials so that their expressive qualities can be effectively highlighted and emphasized.

In our discussion of the similarity between the chorale tune *Aus tiefer Not schrei ich zu dir* and the answer form of the ground-theme inversion, we observed that both musical structures stress the pathopoetic half-step figure.[3] We also observed how the tonal answer of the ground-theme inversion indirectly institutes chromatic motion through the use of a double inflection (c♮ vs. c♯).[4]

Example 33 presents the opening measures of Contrapunctus III. The c♯ in the answer's eighth-note closing figure (measure 4, tenor) is transformed only two pitches later back into c♮. This second set of double inflections found closer together this time (than the set found completely inside the answer) is immediately followed by the two half-step pairs b♮-bb and a-g♯. Chromatic motion is, therefore, only gradually introduced into the texture. In Bach's vocal music, such chromatic passages are regularly associated with texts relating to "sin" and "human frailty."[5] The use of such chromaticism in Bach can be interpreted (in the Christian sense) as belonging to the realm of *Dasein.* The answer's pathopoetic returning-tone figure (e-f-e) also shares these same expressive implications.

---

[2] It should be recalled that the pathopoetic returning-tone figure is found at the midpoint of the ground-theme inversion. This figure also contains the pitches B and A of the B-A-C-H sphere. See chapter 1.

[3] See chapter 5; especially Ex. 25, pp.47-50.

[4] See Ex. 26. Note that the c♮ is formed in the course of an ascending melodic line and the c♯ in the course of a descending line.

[5] See chapter 1, p.10.

The Art of Fugue

EXAMPLE 33

Beginning of Contrapunctus III

Bach had already prepared this chromaticism through a double inflection, which occurs in the countervoice to the final subject entry in Contrapunctus II (Ex. 34, alto). This earlier passage contains nearly the same chromatic materials as the answer in Contrapunctus III.

EXAMPLE 34

Similarity of chromatic materials between Contrapunctus II and IV

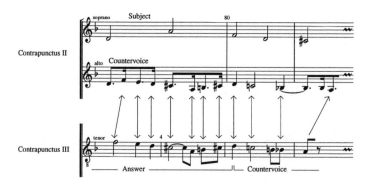

Bach added the section containing this final entry to the Berlin Autograph sometime before engraving the plates for the printed edition.[6] There is a logical reason for this addition, however. In the Berlin Autograph, the fugue which would later be published as Contrapunctus II actually followed the fugue that would be published as Contrapunctus III. When Bach decided to change the order of these two fugues, he probably added the seven extra measures to the end of the Berlin Autograph version in order to prepare the following chromatic fugue better. According to my interpretation, the dotted-note punctuation of Contrapunctus II expresses the statement, "I desire." Because of the chromaticism at its end, however, perhaps one might better say that Contrapunctus II expresses the idea, "I desire—nevertheless, I am."

We shall now return again to the beginning of Contrapunctus III (Ex. 33) in order to examine the countervoice (measures 5-9, tenor) more closely. To begin with, the diminished-seventh chord associated with the middle of the ground theme is once again implied (measure 7, downbeat) and then successively filled in and completed at the midpoints of the next two entries of the theme (measures 11 and 17).

The contrapuntal-nudge figure is also associated with this entry of the countervoice. When the pitch d enters (measure 5, alto), a dissonance is created against the tenor c♮. This dissonance requires that the tenor move downward into the consonant b♮. The entry of the b♭ (measure 7, alto) creates a dissonance against the tenor's tied-over c♯, requiring that the tenor move upward into d. Similarly, the entry of the half note f (measure 8, alto) against the tied-over e (tenor) requires that the tenor resolve, after a leap and three intervening eighth notes, downward into d.

In Example 33, the first five pitches of the countervoice, labeled figure a, lie within a perfect fourth. This figure consists of a syncopated motive α and a pair of chromatic pitches labeled motive β. Motive α presents a "deviation" from the normal metric stress, while motive β is a "departure" from the basic order of the diatonic. Both motives α and β are then superimposed, producing a four-pitch chromatic scale segment (⌐⌐⌐). As we discussed earlier, this chromatic segment is the basic structure from which the B-A-C-H sphere is formed.

In measure six, a new pattern labeled figure b appears. Figure b is derived from the thematic eighth-note figure, but this time its first and last pitches form the interval of a diminished fourth (g♯-c). Figure b is then overlapped with an

---

[6] [Translator's note: Though he did not live to complete the task, it is known that Bach personally supervised the engraving of most of the work. The discrepancies between the Berlin Autograph and the final engraved version is evidence, at least here in the early movements of the work, that Bach further developed his concept of the work between the time of the Berlin Autograph and the time that the engraving was done. The dotted-note fugue, known since the first publication of *The Art of Fugue* as Contrapunctus II, ended in the Berlin Autograph version with whole notes on the first beat of measure 78 (the final soprano pitch was c♯).]

ascending variant of figure a. Though there is still a perfect fourth between its starting and ending pitches, the basic pattern of half and whole-steps is different in the ascending version than in the original descending version. The ascending version of figure a also contains the chromatic half-step pair c♮-c♯. Further, the chromatic motive β is superimposed on the syncopated motive α, producing the hybrid motive α/β. The tied-over quarter note (e) is then inserted across the bar line between measures seven and eight, separating the end of the ascending form of figure a from the next statement of figure b. If we add the tied note e to the preceding f (last note of figure a), another syncopated motive α is produced, which picks up the same half-step relationship found at the melodic climax of the answer in measure three (e-f-e).

The meticulous attention to detail in this countervoice is remarkable. Whether from the unfolding of its characteristic chromaticism, from its thematically derived eighth-note patterns, or from syncopation and pathopoetic emphasis (applied sometimes to one motive and sometimes to another), we can begin to perceive its basic expressive nature. It is as though the countervoice is saying, "I am imperfect and contrary to fundamental order. I am sinful and I suffer." Seen in this light, the expressive content of the countervoice is even more important than the compositional techniques from which it is constructed. Furthermore, it could be more than just a coincidence that this countervoice is the first true countersubject to be employed in *The Art of Fugue*. In fact, it is present against nearly all of the twelve subject entries in Contrapunctus III. It can be argued that Bach composed this material to represent (both literally and figuratively) the impossibility of self-redemption—the very essence of the "human condition" in the Christian understanding. Thus, the countervoice also seems to reflect the basic expressive nature of Contrapunctus III, which I have interpreted with the phrase "I [Bach] am."

Additional evidence in support of my interpretation is provided by the observation that the subject of Contrapunctus III appears in several variations within the fugue. Once past the exposition, where the subject and answer are formed out of the inversion of the ground theme, the subject, in its next three entries (measures: 23, soprano; 29, tenor; 35, tenor), takes on the rhythmically syncopated character of the countersubject. This syncopated variant of the ground theme (Ex. 35a) was also foreshadowed in Contrapunctus II (measure 69, tenor), but here in Contrapunctus III, it contains an extra changing-tone figure and several additional passing tones.

After two more entries of the original subject (measures 43, soprano; 51, bass), a second thematic variant emerges (measure 55, alto). This second variant (Ex. 35b) is actually quite similar to the first (Ex. 35a), except that now the syncopation, characterisitic of the first variant, is shoved a quarter note backwards producing an unsyncopated dotted-note rhythm. A new type of syncopation, however, is applied to the climax pitch and the descending scale passage which immediately follows (measure 57). In the second variant, both the change to unsyncopated dotted notes and the new type of syncopation at the climax tend to strengthen the pathopoetic character of the pitch b♭.

EXAMPLE 35

Subject variants in Contrapunctus III

The last of the three subject variants appears in measure 58 (soprano). This variant (Ex. 35c) is nearly identical with the second (Ex. 35b), except that this time a chromatic scale segment appears near its end. Although the pitch a tends to break up the direct chromatic motion of the line, the four chromatically related pitches of the scale segment definitely belong to the B-A-C-H sphere.

After an examination of these three subject variants, the question still remains: are the many variations of the ground theme in *The Art of Fugue* motivated only by musical considerations, or could they also be motivated by different expressive requirements?

Rhetorical Figures

We have already discussed a number of musical-rhetorical figures from this era (e.g., polysyndeton, gradatio, pathopoeia, passus duriusculus, etc.). Such devices represent particular sentiments in a rather straightforward manner, and their meanings are quite specifically defined. Frequently, even the name of the figure itself will describe its meaning. For example, the diminished fourth is often called *quarta falsa* (false fourth), *quarta deficiens* (deficient fourth), or *saltus duriusculus* (a harsh leap). In vocal music, a rhetorical figure can become even more specifically defined when it appears in repeated association with a particular text. Rhetorical figures can also be present in a nonvocal work, however, even when there is no textual reference to clarify its meaning.

Over one hundred specifically named musical figures were compiled and handed down by the composition teachers of the Baroque era. Many of these devices were named after common figures of speech, important to the study of rhetoric (e.g., polysyndeton and gradatio), while others were named after particular musical events or processes (e.g., passus duriusculus or saltus duriusculus). The study of such figures, however, is not limited only to those handed down by teachers of composition. Any distinguishable musical feature, remarkable event or compositional technique employed in the music of this era can, in certain circumstances, be considered a rhetorical device. For example, a particularly emphasized ostinato or syncopated motive may be considered such a figure, and the discant clausula in third subject of the closing fugue (c#-d) can even qualify as a rhetorical figure, because of its connection to the pitches B-A-C-H.

Whether the rhetorical figure is well-known and closely defined or a particularly emphasized musical event, it tends to function as a departure from the norm, an embellishment, a source of creative energy, or an agent of expression. The goal of these figures is to imitate and portray extramusical concepts by musical means. The process of imitation follows the principle of partial conformance as it attempts to create an expressive analogy between a musical figure and a specific object or concept. For example, the interval of a diminished fifth, considered incomplete, artificial, and erroneous in traditional counterpoint, may be used as a rhetorical figure which seeks to represent human imperfection *(Dasein).*

In Baroque-era music, rhetorical figures and what they represent are linked together by strong analogies. In other words, a rhetorical figure directly communicates its meaning through some perceptually identifiable characteristic. In contrast, a purely extramusical symbol cannot immediately reveal its meaning. For example, both the pitch-letter symbolism of the B-A-C-H motto and the alpha-numeric symbolism of the number fourteen require a certain foreknowledge. An accurate understanding of Baroque musical figures demands a thorough knowledge of time-honored rhetorical practices and an intelligent approach to music history.

The widespread employment of rhetorical figures in contrapuntal works began and ended in the Baroque era. These practices, which had gradually evolved since the end of the sixteenth century, conformed to contemporary aesthetic demands for a musical expression that was highly dependent on text. It was believed that a close association between text and musical figures would make it possible to understand and teach the art of musical expression better. The art of musical-rhetorical figuration was also dependent upon the rational rules of counterpoint, however. In fact, counterpoint provided the background medium upon which rhetorical figures were applied and emphasized.

After the middle of the eighteenth century however, two major developments caused the use of rhetorical figures to fall from favor: 1) contrapuntal compositions and the "rules" of counterpoint were being gradually superseded by newer procedures which were regulated by functional harmony; and 2) composers were beginning to think in terms of individualistic and independently conceived "aesthetics" for their works. In other words, composers of the mid-eighteenth century became interested in writing music whose expressive meaning could be psychologically perceived and understood without the aid of external rhetoric.

Bach, however, considered the expressive use of musical-rhetorical figures to be as important as the art of counterpoint itself, and indeed, where his music is most pregnant with meaning, rhetorical figuration is often richest and most intense. Good examples of Bach's highly colorful rhetorical figuration can be found in the *Three-Part Invention in F minor;* the *Orgelbüchlein* chorale, *"Durch Adams Fall ist ganz verderbt; "*and the *Crucifixus* from the B-Minor Mass. *The Art of Fugue* should also be included with these other works, since it is in no way inferior in rhetorical content, despite the fact that *The Art of Fugue* was [primarily] composed to demonstate Bach's understanding of contrapuntal craft.

To demonstrate Bach's use of rhetorical figures in *The Art of Fugue,* we shall now turn our attention to a short excerpt from the first episode of Contrapunctus III (Ex. 36). Like our earlier quotation from the exposition of this fugue (Ex. 33), this episode also exhibits the same symbolic chromaticism that we interpreted earlier as belonging to the sphere of human imperfection ("I am").

An important compositional texture appears in this episode [and also in a later appearing episode; measures 39-42], which is really quite different from the one employed in the rest of the fugue. In the exposition, subsequent entries, and other short episodes, individual voices either carry the subject or are constructed to be relatively equal in importance. In the first episode, however, the texture actually changes to reflect a trio sonatalike structure; that is, the soprano and alto share an obligatolike melodic texture, while the bass is constructed from contrasting accompanimental material.

The bass-line motive of this passage is derived from the thematic eighth-note figure. In certain respects, it is also similar to figure b in Example 33. There are two major differences between the thematic eighth-note figure and the complete bass-line motive of the episode, however. Two extra eighth notes are added at the beginning of the thematic eighth-note figure (forming the pitch succession a-bb-a in measure 19); then, a characteristic downward octave leap is added at the end of the figure. Typical of many continuo bass lines, the bass motive in this episode initiates a sequential pattern. Set off from each other by eighth rests, the bass motive and its three following sequences follow a circle-

EXAMPLE 36

First episode of Contrapunctus III

of-fifths progression. This sequence actually facilitates a large-scale modulation from the key of A major to the key of F major [A-D-G-C-F].

The obligatolike soprano and alto exchange two separate motives with each other in every measure of this episode. The first motive (a_1) is constructed from four descending pitches a half step apart. This motive is derived from the beginning of the countersubject (Ex. 33, figure a), from which it takes both its syncopation and its chromaticism. The second motive (c) is constructed from four pitches which are approached and departed by leap. Furthermore, the second pitch of the motive is changed to a dotted quarter note.[7] It should also be observed that the melodic interval of a diminished fourth is always present [in the same voice] between the exchange of the chromatic motive (a_1) and the subsequent leaping motive (c).

---

[7] We have already discussed how the dotted-note figure, tied-note figure and rhythmic syncopation determine the thematic variations that will be applied to later entries of the subject. See p.72.

The expressive content conveyed by this episodic passage bears a striking resemblance to the expression of "human frailty," which was presented earlier by the countersubject. In fact, the same rhetorical figures employed in the countersubject (syncopation, passus duriusculus and quarta falsa or saltus duriusculus) are also emphasized here in the first episode. It is as if Bach were directly associating this episode with the chorale text *Sieh nicht an unser Sünde groß* (Do not look upon our great sinfulness).[8]

Other figures in this passage also reflect the unchanging sinful nature of human existence and the impossibility of self-redemption. The stubborn motific iteration of the bass line takes on an ostinatolike character,[9] while the eighth rests between statements of the bass motive are examples of the rhetorical figure *tmesis* (cutting apart). It is possible that these tmesis figures might actually represent the separation of humankind from God. At the same time, the two upper voices, which are constantly twisting around each other, establish a pattern of persistent chromaticism.

This four measure excerpt is a good example of what Walther called "compulsory or treacherous counterpoint" *(contrapunto obligato oder perfidiato).*[10] Walther continues by saying that pieces requiring this kind of compositional expression are characterized by "a stubborn counterpoint, from which nothing is allowed to deviate." In this light, perhaps it is possible that Bach intended the trio sonatalike texture of this episode to intrude stubbornly upon the otherwise standard fugal textures employed in Contrapunctus III.

The music of this episode speaks through its figures, and these figures seem to say, "I am contrary to the order of things and sinful." In addition, out of the bass ostinato figure comes the sentiment, "I am mired in this sinful condition and can find no way of escape by my own power"—*Sieh nicht an unser Sünde groß / sprich uns derselb aus Gnaden los* (Do not look upon our great sinfulness / forgive us out of Thy mercy). It is for the same reason that the B-A-C-H motto in the closing fugue requires the addition of the pitches c#-d.

B-A-C-H

The highly chromatic Contrapunctus III finds a later counterpart in Contrapunctus XI. As opposed to Contrapunctus III, which is a simple fugue,

---

[8] [Translator's note: From verse six of *Wenn wir in höchsten Nöten sein.*]

[9] [Translator's note: An ostinato is "a clearly defined phrase that is repeated persistently, usually in immediate succession, throughout a composition or a section."—Willi Apel, ed., *Harvard Dictionary of Music,* second ed. (Cambridge, Mass., Belknap Press, 1969): 634.]

[10] Johann Gottfried Walther, *Musikalisches Lexikon oder Musikalische Bibliothek,* 1732.

Contrapunctus XI is a fugue on two subjects and two countersubjects. In addition to its highly chromatic nature, Contrapunctus XI also functions as the final movement in the group of multisubject fugues (Table 2, p.114).

Contrapunctus XI and Contrapunctus VIII are also closely related. Contrapunctus VIII, a three-voice fugue on two subjects and one countersubject, functions as the opening fugue in the group of fugues on multiple subjects. In the Berlin Autograph, the fugue that would become Contrapunctus XI directly follows the fugue that would become Contrapunctus VIII. In the final printed version of the work, however, these two fugues provide the outside framework for two additional double fugues (Contrapuncti IX and X).

Contrapunctus XI shares both its two subjects and one of its two countersubjects with Contrapunctus VIII. In Contrapunctus XI, however, the subjects are presented in a different order. As we will see, this new order of subjects is crucial to the expressive content of Contrapunctus XI. Another important difference in Contrapunctus XI is the addition of a second countersubject. This addition demonstrates the process of ever-increasing fugal complexity. Contrapunctus XI also utilizes both normal and inverted forms of its two subjects. The two forms of the subject and the two countersubjects are then combined with each other in ways that demonstrate a number of important contrapuntal techniques.

Contrapunctus XI is divided into two major parts. The first part is eighty-nine measures long, whereas the second part is ninety-five measures (measures 90-184). The first part is further broken down into three smaller sections, each of which contains a partial fugue, while the second part generally treats entries of subject and countersubject more freely.

Part one of Contrapunctus XI begins with a partial fugue, whose subject is based on a variation of the ground theme. This variation (Ex. 37) is characterized by a nearly constant use of eighth notes, the insertion of two extra pitches (x) into the basic ground-theme pattern, and above all, by the presence of an eighth rest at the beginning of each measure. The aural impression that these rests make clearly belong to the musical-rhetorical figure *suspiratio*.

Suspiratio is described in Baroque treatises as a rhetorical figure representing "sighing and moaning." Since the opening subject of the first part of this fugue employs this figure, we shall label this subject the suspiratio variation. It was also previously employed in Contrapunctus VIII, but only in its inverted form (measures 94-98). Its introduction here at the beginning of Contrapunctus XI is clearly the goal of its earlier introduction and development. The suspiratio variation, with its sighing motives set off by rests, figuratively represents the lamenting "I" of human existence. Furthermore, if we include in the total the two extra pitches (x) described above, this subject variant contains fourteen pitches. It is not difficult to interpret the number symbolism here— Bach himself is the "I".

EXAMPLE 37

Contrapunctus XI: Part I; the subject of the first partial fugue

In measure eight, the alto countervoice presents a syncopated figure against the final measure of the answer (Ex. 38a).[11] From this point on, such encroachments against the underlying metric order play an ever increasing role in Contrapunctus XI. Upon the completion of the answer (measure 9), the soprano line moves immediately into a short chromatic scale segment. The contrapuntal association of this chromatic segment with the entry of the suspiratio variation (measure 9, bass) heightens and sharply defines the rhetorical symbolism. This passage represents the "burden of sin."

EXAMPLE 38a

Contrapunctus XI: Part I, first partial fugue

As we have discussed, chromatic motion was introduced into the cycle by the answer form of the inverted ground theme in Contrapunctus III. In Contrapunctus XI, however, chromatic motion is motivated by the expressive nature of the suspiratio variation itself. As a further indication of its rhetorical context, the suspiratio variation also pulls the passus-duriusculus figure along with it. Following the exposition (measures 1-17), the suspiratio variation enters only one more time in the first partial fugue (soprano, measure 21). Near the end of this entry, the alto countervoice accompanies the subject with a descending

---

[11] [Translator's note: The alto and bass voices were added to the author's original excerpt in Ex. 38a, so that the relationship between the three voices could be more easily visualized.]

chromatic passage which lies within the perfect fourth d-a (Ex. 38b).[12] This chromatic scale segment (passus duriusculus) prefigures the soon-to-follow chromatic countersubject of the second partial fugue (Ex. 41, measures 28-30, soprano).

EXAMPLE 38b

Contrapunctus XI: Part I, first partial fugue

The second partial fugue of Contrapunctus XI (beginning measure 27) introduces a subject based on inversion of the ground theme. This same subject, in its noninverted form, first appeared at the beginning of Contrapunctus VIII. Therefore, we shall first examine the noninverted subject (Ex. 39) before discussing the inversion. The noninverted form of the subject not only appears in Contrapunctus VIII, but also twice in Contrapunctus XI (measures 57-60, soprano; 68-71, bass).

EXAMPLE 39

The Step-leap Subject: beginning of Contrapunctus VIII

This cheerful, dancelike subject, buoyant and full of life, is a mixture of step and leap. It is characterized by a dominating chromatic descent that lies within the interval of a perfect fifth. The chromatic background is interrupted, however, by several upward leaps of a fourth, followed immediately by downward leaps of a fifth. This lively *step-leap* subject, constructed from fourteen pitches (although perhaps only coincidentally), not only exposes the B-A-C-H sphere, but is also the first "newly fashioned" subject in *The Art of Fugue*.

---

[12] [Translator's note: Although the author does not include Example 38b in his original text, it is included here to illustrate further the author's analysis.]

Is this subject actually new, however? Example 40 shows a possible indirect derivation by way of the countersubject to Contrapunctus III. We have already discussed how chromatic materials in Contrapunctus III relate to and were derived from the ground theme.[13]

EXAMPLE 40

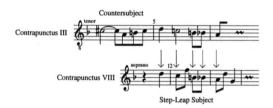

Bach does not allow this chromatic association with the countersubject of Contrapunctus III to conflict with the cheerful, dancelike nature of the step-leap subject in Contrapunctus VIII, but the dark expressive content of the chromatic materials completely dominates the second partial fugue in Contrapunctus XI. In contrast to the opening subject of Contrapunctus VIII, the step-leap subject is first introduced in inverted form in Contrapunctus XI (Ex. 41). In measures 28-30, the inverted subject is immediately set in counterpoint against an ascending chromatic passage (soprano), which is then followed by a descending chromatic line (measures 30-32, bass). This chromaticism appears against the subject with such regularity that it should be considered a countersubject. Indeed, every time that the inverted step-leap subject enters (measures 27-31; 34-38; 43-47), these materials seem to interject their expressive commentary. Chromatic influence is not limited to the countersubject, however, since this same kind of chromaticism also permeates the episodes and, indeed, the rest of the entire fugue.

The third partial fugue (measures 71-89) consists of an exposition whose subject is formed by the inversion of the suspiratio variation (Ex. 42). At the beginning of this section, the soprano and alto present two sighlike suspension figures (measures 71-73) at the point where the subject enters in the tenor. The second of these sigh figures functions as the resolution of a diminished-seventh chord (measure 72, last quarter). Out of this resolution, the soprano proceeds into a sequence of pitches which closely resembles the B-A-C-H motto, while the rhetorical tmesis figure can be observed in the separated ("cut-apart") half steps of the bass line. Chromaticism and syncopated motives continue to dominate the rest of the third partial fugue, which ends with a single "sighing" suspension figure (measure 89, alto).

---

[13][Translator's note: see pp.69-73]

EXAMPLE 41

Contrapunctus XI: Part I, second partial fugue

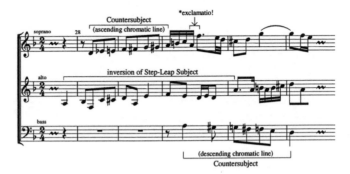

Note: the ascending chromatic passage within the perfect fifth d-a (soprano) leads into a rhetorical figure called *exclamatio* (exclamation). In this example exclamatio is represented by the upward leap of a sixth in measure 30.

EXAMPLE 42

Contrapunctus XI: Part I, third partial fugue

To summarize, in the first part of Contrapunctus XI the sighing, inverted suspiratio theme (with its interpolated rests), sighlike suspension figures, tmesis figures, and the two diminished fifths (*quintae deficientes*) of the diminished-seventh chord all share the same expressive idea (*Dasein*) as the B-A-C-H motto itself.

Part two of Contrapunctus XI begins with the same inverted form of the lively step-leap subject (measure 89, bass) employed earlier, in part one, as the subject of the second partial fugue in part one (Ex. 43). This time, however, the subject is not accompanied by the same countersubject material as before, but rather by a new countersubject. This highly agitated and chromatic second countersubject is constructed primarily from sixteenth-note patterns that contain several pitch repetitions and suspension figures. The musical tension produced by this countersubject is intensified by its appearance in stretto (compare measure 90, alto; with measure 89, tenor). The alto entrance of this countersubject starts on b♭, clearly exposing the B-A-C-H motto, and since this same intervallic pattern is also found beginning on pitches other than b♭, the purely motific value of the B-A-C-H motto is further strengthened.

EXAMPLE 43

Contrapunctus XI: beginning of Part II

A descending form of this countersubject already appeared in Contrapunctus VIII. Ex. 44 shows how the descending form can be derived from the step-leap subject.

EXAMPLE 44

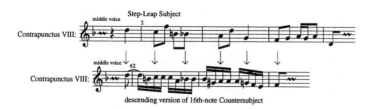

I do not wish to become embroiled in an argument over whether this sixteenth-note passage is actually a third subject (as many others hold), or only a second countersubject (my opinion). The melodic material of this passage is not thematically precise, however, and it becomes particularly unstable after its second measure. In addition, it never really appears as the subject of a clear fugal exposition, but rather is found throughout part two of Contrapunctus XI in both its ascending and mirrored-descending form. Moreover, this nearly omnipresent melodic material is employed in all possible contrapuntal combinations against the subjects and itself. There is little doubt that Bach intended the pitches b-a-c-h to be symbolic here, though the B-A-C-H motto appears without its following discant clausula figure.

Contrapunctus XI can be described as a fugue which summarizes nearly all the contrapuntal procedures which have appeared in the preceding fugues. It contains examples of fugue on one subject (part one, first and third partial fugues), on the normal (noninverted) form of a second subject with one countersubject (part one, beginning of second partial fugue), on the inverted form of this second subject with one countersubject (part one, end of second partial fugue), and finally, on two subjects and two countersubjects (part two). Part two of this fugue also includes stretto, thematic inversion and complete invertibility (voice exchange) of all materials which occur in counterpoint. In addition, part two also contains two spots in which there is a simultaneous entry of the subject in its normal form against the subject in inversion (measures 158-62, soprano and alto; 164-68, tenor and bass). This thematic mirroring antici-pates the complete mirroring of all fugal materials which will occur in the immediately following contrapuncti (the mirror fugues).

Contrapunctus XI is one of Bach's most texturally dense fugues, but at the same time, also one of his most expressive. This fugue creates the distinct impression that something "full of life" is being placed into a world of "sighing." It expresses "the difficult walk," and communicates a sense of "restlessness and fear."

The musical materials of Contrapunctus XI certainly support this interpre-tation. We have already observed how the lively step-leap subject grew out of the same chromatic ground that characterized Contrapunctus III, and how the chromatic countersubject that accompanies the step-leap subject in the second partial fugue brings additional expressive commentary to the movement; a commentary which culminates later in the anxious stretto entrance of the sixteenth-note countersubject, with its exposed B-A-C-H motto, at the beginning of part two. Like Contrapunctus III, but now more intense and clear in the greater power of its compositional invention, Contrapunctus XI states, "I am." Further, the setting into which the B-A-C-H motto is placed becomes evidence that this "I am" is the composer himself.

Contrapunctus XI also stands at the climax of tension in the cycle, especially if we consider the sudden change of expression that takes place in the contrapuncti that directly follow. In the next two fugues, both the musical materials and their expressive assertions are figuratively cancelled out by their respective mirror-fugue pairs. Similarly, the musical figures representative of sighing, difficulty, and anxiety disappear, as do the stubborn syncopations and diminished intervals. It is as if all of the onerous characteristics of the "human condition" were totally wiped clean by an act of mercy. Indeed, for Christians, the reconciliation of "human nature" with that of the "Divine" is not a matter of human "works," but rather the result of God's mercy. The mirror-fugue contrapuncti in *The Art of Fugue* can, therefore, be considered symbolic of "human sinfulness" vis à vis "divine mercy." This Christian concept of redemption through mercy is also symbolized by the B-A-C-H-C#-D theme itself. The "I" (Bach) seeks union with the Tonic (God) on the ground of mercy alone.

Musical Affections

Both rhetorical figures and affective textures were fundamental devices of musical expression in the Baroque. In fact, these two forms of expression are somewhat difficult to separate, since they freely touch and intersect one another. They do, however, differ somewhat in that musical-rhetorical figures represent specific concrete sentiments, whereas affective musical textures attempt to portray more general emotional states.

In their basic gestures and contours, musical-rhetorical figures attempt to portray concrete objects, attitudes, specific matters or circumstances (e.g., sin, falsehood, mercy or also perhaps the coiling of the serpent, the height of the heavens or the arms of the cross), whereas affective textures attempt to musically portray common states of the human soul (e.g., love, hate, hope, doubt, etc.). Though affective musical textures are less specific in their meanings, they can sometimes be formed out of musical-rhetorical figures. For example, the sighing figure is capable of creating the affection of "longing," passus duriusculus can be connected with the affection of "sadness," the rhetorical ostinato with "stubbornness," and the pathopoetic returning-tone figure with "sorrow."

The art of composing with rhetorical figures exploits the use of a direct analogy between particular types of musical materials and extramusical objects or concepts. The recorded collection of these figures is called *musica poetica*. Freely used by Baroque-era composers, these figures provide distinctive ornamentation intended to embody specific extra-musical associations. Each musical figure is a compositional event which belongs to the poetically objective side of music; that is, it belongs to the artistic raw materials from which a work is constructed. By themselves, however, such figures have either no effect on or are of only secondary importance to the actual "soul" of a work.

On the other hand, the study of affective textures and their employment in Baroque-era compositions is based on an analogy between specific human emotions and particular musical materials. Musical textures were actually classified according to the type of sentiment they conveyed and by the way human emotions reacted to and were moved by them. It must be pointed out, however, that these classified textures were not considered to be mechanical formulas for expression; that is, specific textures were not studied so that a composer could arrive at a set of musical norms and deviations from them. Rather, the study of affections and their associated musical textures was considered a guide to the way certain musical situations influence a listener's emotions. Under no obligation to use affective textures, composers freely employed them as they attempted to associate musical passages with particular emotional states.

Affective musical textures were derived by psychological and mathematical processes. Psychological affections were based on the moods and spirit of life (*humores and spiritus animales*). Depending, of course, upon the personality of the listener, composers attempted to induce particular psychological affections by employing certain kinds of musical textures.[14] On the other hand, mathematically derived affective textures were based on the numerical proportions of harmonic perfection and imperfection which occur within musical intervals.[15] The closer the mathematical proportion of an interval to the ideal of perfection and unity, the greater the implication of joy and contentment; and conversely, the further away an interval is from this ideal, the greater the implication of confusion and sorrow.

The definition and use of affective musical textures actually originated in the Italian and French Renaissance, but they became widely employed in the Baroque era and even beyond. Both affective textures and musical-rhetorical figures were born in the philosophy of humanism and were, for the most part, associated with music from German-speaking lands. However, the use of musical-rhetorical figures was so dependent upon a contrapuntal medium that the displacement of pure counterpoint by more modern musical trends [especially functional harmony] spelled the end of compositional expression based on such figures. In fact, it could be said that Bach's *The Art of Fugue* is the last great work in which rhetorical figures functioned as a principal means of expression.

---

[14] For example, since joy corresponds to an expanded sense of animation within the human spirit, large melodic intervals might be employed, whereas a more contained melody featuring smaller intervals might be used to portray a sense of grief.

[15] [Translator's note: In Pythagorean intonation, the frequencies of the two pitches which form a unison are in the simplest (therefore) most highly consonant proportion of 1:1, whereas (for example) the frequencies of the pitches which form an augmented fourth (tritone) are in the much more complicated and dissonant proportion of 11:4.]

The primary domain of musical affections was the opera, oratorio, and other public music. Unlike rhetorical figures, the use of affective musical textures was not discarded at the end of the Baroque era. Rather, they were gradually absorbed into and ultimately taken over by a new type of musical expression. In the post-Baroque era, composers sought to create highly refined musical textures that could directly influence the mental state of a listener without depending upon any external reference. For this new breed of composer, reliance upon classified musical affections was considered unnecessary, since affective musical textures can only imitate the external gestures of particular psychological states.

Handel's music, especially his public works, relied heavily on musical affections, whereas Bach's music is characterized more by its rhetorical figuration. For that reason, a firm knowledge of rhetorical details is necessary before Bach's music can be fully comprehended. Musical affections, however, are not uncommon in the music of Bach, and we can often discover outspoken affections of joy, sweetness, and sorrow in his works.

To illustrate Bach's use of affective textures in *The Art of Fugue,* let us examine a short passage from the end of the second episode in Contrapunctus IV (Ex. 45). Two musical motives characterize this fugue. The first of the two is the thematic eighth-note figure, which establishes an immediate reference to the ground theme and at the same time functions to provide a forward rhythmic drive. The second motive consists of a descending skip of a third, which, though only gradually introduced in the exposition, completely dominates the materials of the first episode (measures 19-26). The nearly constant employment of the skipping-third motive and the appearance of many exposed major triads are the essential factors that help to fashion the affection of joy in Contrapunctus IV.[16]

The thematic eighth-note figure is also constructed from a pair of interlocking descending thirds (Ex. 45, alto and tenor). Between the thematic eighth-note figure and the skipping-third motive, the interval of a descending third is omnipresent in the texture. This episodic passage sounds complete, lovely, and clear. It reflects a cheerful countenance and radiates a sense of elation springing from joyful confidence.

This example from Contrapunctus IV is quite modern (pre-Classical) in character because of its typical song-form phrase structure. It is actually an eight-measure period constructed from two four-measure phrases (a four-measure antecedent, followed directly by a four-measure consequent).

The antecedent phrase is dominated by the skipping-third motive, which alternates between the soprano and the bass, while the inner voices trade off entries of the thematic eighth-note figure. Note that the tenor imitates the alto an octave lower throughout the antecedent, creating a succession of four pairs of

---

[16] [Translator's note: The consonant interval of a third and the major triad *(chord of nature)* are considered mathematically based affections here.]

EXAMPLE 45

Second episode of Contrapunctus IV

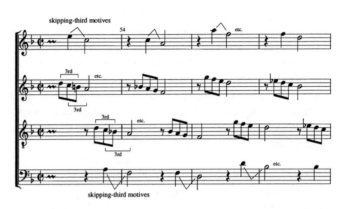

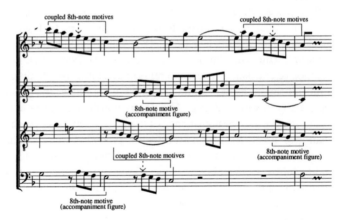

thematic eighth-note figures. Both the quarter-note skipping thirds and the thematic eighth-note figures are presented in such a way that the measure is clearly defined as the basic unit of the periodic structure.[17]

In the consequent phrase, the eighth-note motive takes over the foreground from the quarter-note skipping-third motive. Here, two eighth-note figures are actually coupled together to form an octave-long descending scale passage (soprano: 57-58, 60-61; tenor and bass: 58-59). Note that the second halves of these descending scales are also accompanied in parallel thirds by other thematic

---

[17] [Translator's note: This straightforward periodic structure supports the concept of orderliness, and thus the affection of joy.]

eighth-note motives.[18] Sensibly, the bass is allowed to rest (measures 59-60) before entering with the subject (measure 61).

Contrapunctus IV is the last fugue in the opening group of the cycle. Like Contrapunctus III before it, Contrapunctus IV is a fugue on the inversion of the ground theme. The subjects of both Contrapuncti III and IV employ the pathopoetic pitch succession a-b♭-a, which so richly characterizes the "human condition." However, the expressive content in Contrapunctus IV does not represent the anguished statement "I am," rather it implies a joyful confidence that seems to say, "I will become." This confident character is maintained in spite of the fact that the opening motive of the countervoice the closely repeated eighth-note figure b♭-a-g♯-a [not shown in Ex. 45; see measures 5-7, soprano] and the rising chromatic scale segment within a perfect fourth (measures 83-85, bass) actually belong to the realm of the pathopoetic.

The analogy between the musical materials and the statement, "I will become," is strengthened when we consider that this fugue begins again on the tonic pitch d (subject form of the inverted ground theme),[19] and is further strengthened when we consider that the closing fugue of the cycle establishes a similar expressive character.

The musical materials in the coda of Contrapunctus IV also support and help clarify the expressive interpretation we have applied to the episodic section shown in Ex. 45. In addition to sharing the same basic spirit and affection of joy with the episode, the coda of Contrapunctus IV also contains an emphatic repetition of the discant clausula (c♯-d; measures 133-38, soprano),[20] which is then contrapuntally connected to the pitches of the B-A-C-H motto (measures 135-36, tenor).[21] Although Contrapunctus IV does not appear in the Berlin Autograph, it is included in that portion of the first printed version which Bach himself supervised. The possibility that Bach added this fugue to the cycle in order to clarify the rhetorical statements which we claim to recognize in *The Art of Fugue* is thereby further supported.

---

[18] [Translator's note: Actually parallel tenths; parallel thirteenths (sixths) in measures 57-58. These consonant parallel intervals can also be considered a mathematically based affection.]

[19] [Translator's note: It should be remembered that Contrapunctus III began on the pitch a with the answer form of the theme.]

[20] See Ex. 21.

[21] [Translator's note: This supports the author's premise that Bach intended the material of the coda to represent the rhetorical statement: "[alas] I am, but there is joy in the hope of what I shall become."]

The Dramatic

There are many places in *The Art of Fugue* where the expressive nature of rhetorical figures and musical affections becomes highly dramatic. From such dramatic spots come profound and exciting revelations of the depth and pathos of Bach's character. Such revelations are not unlike the impressions we gain from his personal writings, his portrait, the sermons he preaches in his cantatas, or the personality he reveals in his keyboard and organ works.

The end of Contrapunctus I comes to mind as a particularly good example of such dramatic action. Above the punctuating harmonic texture of the inner voices (after measure 60), the soprano proceeds with a variation of the thematic eighth-note motive which winds its way upward into the quarter-note half-step progression eb-d-c♯ (measures 62-63) and then directly into the *exclamatio* figure c♯-a (measure 63). Beneath the exclamatio figure, the bass supplies a pedal point (a), which establishes a dissonant impetus for the soprano's gradual octave descent (measures 63-66). The pedal point is then followed (measures 66-69, bass) by a series of upward-leaping intervals (g-d, c-f, e-a, g-c), whose sequential dominant-tonic relationships function to bleed off some of the harmonic tension which had accumulated in the previous three measures. At the conclusion of these sequences, the bass line smoothly resolves into the half note bb (measure 70), while the soprano leaps downward into the third quarter of the measure, sounding the framing pitches (bb-c♯) of the c♯ diminished-seventh chord [vii^{o7}].

Suddenly, the musical texture is broken off by an abrupt grand pause, followed by a single six-four chord [i$^6_4$] and another grand pause. This second grand pause leads directly to a g♯ diminished-seventh chord [vii^{o7}/V], which immediately proceeds into a standard d-minor cadence formula [i$^6_4$-V^7]. This cadence formula then resolves (measure 74) into a complete d-major tonic triad (*picardy third* [i^3]).

It is as though Bach wanted this dramatic textural caesura to represent the subject's desire to break free from the burden of the ever-present tie figures which characterize the rest of the fugue. As was mentioned in chapter 5, it was not until after the composition of the Berlin Autograph that Bach added the coda (measures 74-78) which appears in the final printed version. It was probably during this time that he also grasped the full dramatic significance of the caesura in this passage.

The five-voice coda of Contrapunctus VII (Ex. 46) provides another example of the dramatic in *The Art of Fugue*. Contrapunctus VII is the last of the three counterfugues (Contrapuncti V, VI, VII). The final subject entry in Contrapunctus VII (measures 50-58, first soprano) is also the last statement of the augmented dotted-note subject. This thematic variant appears a number of times, during the course of the fugue, like a solemn cantus firmus. The last note (d) of this entry (measure 58) initially appears as a member of the unstable tonic six-four chord [i$^6_4$]. This d is held, however, while the underlying harmony is bridged-over to a g# diminished-seventh chord [vii^{o7}/V] by sixteenth-note figuration in both the second soprano and bass.[22] The alto and tenor voices rest during this change of harmony.

EXAMPLE 46

Coda of Contrapunctus VII

_____

[22] The connecting function of the thematic eighth-note motive is taken over by the sixteenth-note figure in Contrapunctus VII.

When all five voices resume again (measure 58, last half of the second quarter), the resulting punctuation of the diminished-seventh chord [vii^{o7}/V] sounds remarkably like a continuo entrance in a secco recitative. Indeed, the first soprano proceeds directly out of this punctuated sonority into a solo quasi-recitative passage which is exactly fourteen notes in length. The discant clausula figure (c#-d) is stated twice within this passage. After the resolution of the second discant clausula, the d of the first soprano is again absorbed into an unstable tonic six-four chord [i$^6_4$] (measure 59, second quarter).

Above the quasi-recitative material, which is then continued forward in the second soprano, the first soprano states the discant clausula figure a third time in longer more heavily stressed quarter notes. The alto then picks up the quasi-recitative, while the first soprano begins a new fourteen-note segment [measures 60-61] in which a fourth statement of the discant clausula is set up. This time, however, it is foiled by an eighth-note chromatic descent (c#-c♮). This last quasi-recitative passage then moves through another diminished-seventh chord [vii^{o7}] (measure 61, second quarter) which resolves downward into the bright picardy third (f#) of the final d-major triad [i^3].

The duality between the objective and the subjective is clearly audible and visible near the ends of both Contrapunctus I and Contrapunctus VII. Both fugues contain solemn cantus firmuslike subjects (objective) and moments of highly dramatic action (subjective).

8

Variation

Alongside the various procedures of counterpoint and the model of fugal form, variation technique plays a vital role in *The Art of Fugue*. The term *variation* is most frequently associated with a set of melodic re-shaping procedures *(Gestaltvariationen)*, where a theme, though somewhat altered in each subsequent statement, remains clearly recognizable throughout. In our discussion, however, the term variation will also be applied to those processes by which a theme can be transformed into completely new melodic ideas *(thematic metamorphosis)*. Within these two broad categories, some of the more important procedures of variation in *The Art of Fugue* are: 1) the reduction or compression of musical materials, specifically, the construction of new materials by combining the pitches of the ground theme's normal and inverted forms; 2) the formation of new melodic patterns out of one or more of the ground theme's characteristic motives; and 3) and the interpolation of additional pitches between the tones of the ground theme. The third procedure is especially important in the development of the countersubjects.[1]

Since Bach develops the fundamental materials of the ground theme along new lines in each succeeding movement, it is as important to understand his processes of thematic variation as it is to study the ground theme itself. Bach's multifaceted approach to monothematicism in *The Art of Fugue* supports the aesthetic idea, mentioned earlier, that everything should proceed from and return to the same source. Although this aesthetic connection cannot be absolutely proved, there are certainly clear connections between the musical materials of the normal and inverted forms of the ground theme and all of the subjects in the cycle.

---

[1] [Translator's note: Compare, for example, the inverted ground theme (III:1-5, tenor) with the countersubject that immediately follows (III:5-8, tenor).]

Certainly, Bach would have known the rhetorical significance of his thematic variations as well as he did their technical possibilities. Since rhetorical devices have been at work on all other levels in *The Art of Fugue,* it is unlikely that Bach would have missed the opportunity to apply rhetorical significance to each variation of the ground theme. *The Art of Fugue,* with all of its thematic mutations and transformations, is not only rich in texture, but also in variety of expression. There seems to be a conscious change of statement and point of reference in each newly derived variation of the ground theme, and if we follow our interpretation, it is as if Bach intended to focus on some unique aspect of the relationship between *Sein* and *Dasein* in each of these variations.

The ground theme is actually altered on several distinct levels. On the most obvious and self-explanatory level, these changes are associated with the basic requirements of fugal form. These form-dependent variations, which account for the majority of the thematic alterations in the cycle, include the tonally adjusted answer and its inversion, as well as the inversion form of the ground theme itself. Also belonging to this category are the slight thematic alterations which occur when a ground-theme derived subject (or answer) is stated in or modulates to another key. Also to be considered are those changes introduced by augmentation and diminution in the counterfugues.[2]

The second level of thematic variation found in *The Art of Fugue* consists of the reshaping procedures *(Gestaltvariationen)* mentioned above. In this type of variation, the theme is often subjected to changes of meter or other rhythmic alterations. Furthermore, the normal relationship between the pitches of the ground theme is frequently altered by the addition of interpolated notes or ornaments which form returning-tone or neighboring-tone figures around the pitches of the original ground theme.

In Examples 47-53, we shall not only examine the thematic variation that occurs, but also attempt to interpret the rhetorical meaning associated with each change. As each example is discussed, one must remember that these variants did not just suddenly appear, but, rather, were musically prepared and announced at some earlier stage in the work. Some of the changes actually seem to have evolved over a very long period of time before they were transformed into the mature thematic variations shown in these examples. In such cases, specific moments in the evolutionary process can also have great rhetorical and expressive importance.[3]

---

[2] [Translator's note: Counterfugues *(Gegenfuge)* are those fugues where both normal and inverted forms of the subject are present (Contrapuncti V-VII; see Table 2, p.114).]

[3] This supports the idea that everything new must be derived from what already exists.

The process of ground-theme variation begins quite early in *The Art of Fugue.* With the first entry of the subject in Contrapunctus II (Ex. 47), the thematic eighth-note figure is changed into a pattern of dotted eighth and sixteenth notes. This rhythmic variation was prepared, in rudimentary fashion, by the dotted quarter and eighth-note figures which occur in Contrapunctus I.[4]

Beginning as a half-measure anacrusis at the end of the subject, this dotted-note motive charges Contrapunctus II with a driving willful energy which becomes further strengthened when the motive shifts to a strong metrical position and expands to fill an entire bar (measure 5). After this point, with the exception of the tied notes (e.g., Ex. 47, measures 5-6, bass,) the dotted-eighth and sixteenth-note figures are employed on every beat throughout the remainder of the fugue.[5] As we have already discussed, the expression in Contrapunctus II is completely different from that of Contrapunctus I, and it is out of these differences that we have applied the interpretive labels, "It is" (Contrapunctus I) and "I desire" (Contrapunctus II).[6]

EXAMPLE 47

Beginning of Contrapunctus II

---

[4] [Translator's note: The unsyncopated dotted-quarter and eighth-note figure enters quite early in Contrapunctus I (measure 10, alto). This figure then gradually takes on more and more importance until its use climaxes in the middle of the movement (measures 35-40, soprano).]

[5] Special attention and a conscious exertion of energy must be applied to these dotted-note figures during performance.

[6] It should be recalled that the major elements of expression in Contrapunctus I are tied-note suspensions and contrapuntal-nudge figures.

There is a relatively minor variation of the ground theme in Contrapunctus II, but a much more substantial reshaping of the theme takes place in the opening measures of Contrapunctus V (Ex. 48). This variant appears in both normal and inverted forms. Moreover, it is employed as the subject in all three of the counterfugues (Contrapuncti V-VII), where it also enters in augmentation and diminution.[7] Two major features of this variant are its three dotted quarter notes, and its two eighth-note passing tones (inserted between the second and third, and third and fourth pitches of the ground theme).

There is a similarity between the dotted notes of this variant and the dotted-note figure at the end of the subject in Contrapunctus II. Furthermore, both the second fugue of the opening group (simple fugues), and the initial fugue of the second group (counterfugues) contain dotted-note alteration in their subjects. Two interpolated eighth-note passing tones bring the total number of notes in the subject of Contrapunctus V to fourteen. This may not be totally coincidental, since the interpretation of this number as a symbol helps confirm the relationship of the subject to the rhetorical "I" (Bach).

EXAMPLE 48

Subject (normal form) of Contrapunctus V

The statement, "I desire," is intensified in the middle fugue of the second group (Contrapunctus VI). The recurrence of the dotted-eighth and sixteenth-note figure at the end of the subject (measure 4, bass), as well as its appearance in contrary motion (measure 5, soprano) are clear references back to Contrapunctus II. The influence of these dotted-note figures on Contrapunctus VI is further increased by the accompanying thirty-second-note patterns.[8] The rhetorical "I" is also present here in the midst of this dotted-note figuration, but this time the "I" is represented not as a pure-number symbol, but by the tones of the B-A-C-H sphere (refer again to Ex. 18, measures 4-6, soprano). We have already

---

[7] This same variant also appears in its inverted form as one of the two subjects in Contrapunctus XI.

[8] Both dotted rhythms and quick-note ornamentation are typical of the "French-style" Baroque overture.

discussed how the ground theme was altered to form the three scalar variants of the subject in Contrapunctus III (p.73).

The next new variant of the ground theme is found in both Contrapunctus VIII and Contrapunctus XI (Ex. 49), the first and last fugues of the third group of contrapuncti (fugues on multiple subjects). This thematic variant borrows its fourteen-pitch length from the subject of the counterfugue group, but then substitutes the "sighing" figure, with its eighth notes and eighth rests, for the dotted-note rhythm found in the counterfugues.

EXAMPLE 49

Opening Subject of Contrapunctus XI

Suspiratio Theme

This theme is also employed (in its inverted form) as the second subject of Contrapunctus VIII; see VIII: mm. 94-98, alto.

If we examine a further thematic variation, which also appears in Contrapunctus XI, it becomes quite obvious that the suspiratio variation of the ground theme was rhetorically motivated, and that this subject was fashioned to serve the chromatic side of the work. Starting at the anacrusis to measure 155 (Ex. 50), suspiratio figures and passus duriusculus (bass) are contrapuntally combined with "sighing" suspension figures (upper voices).

EXAMPLE 50

Contrapunctus XI

The subject of the first pair of mirror fugues (Contrapunctus XIIa,b) is also a reshaped variation of the ground theme (Ex. 51).[9] We have already discussed how the total mirroring of materials at this point in the cycle relates to the Christian concept of "mercy" (chapter 7, p.85). It should, therefore, not be surprising that the thematic variation in the first pair of mirror fugues also implies a similar rhetorical motivation. The thematically reshaped subject of Contrapunctus XIIa,b is thoroughly diatonic. Entering for the first time in the bass at the beginning of Contrapunctus XIIa, the subject establishes a strong tonal foundation for the entire fugue.[10] This strong fundamental entry also establishes a sudden change in the basic meter of the entire work. In fact, the only occurrence of triple meter in *The Art of Fugue* occurs here in Contrapunctus XIIa,b. The change to triple meter *(tempus perfectum)* could be a rhetorical reference to the perfection of the Holy Trinity, and the subject with its swinging rhythm and two-part structure brings an air of peacefulness to this first mirror fugue.[11]

EXAMPLE 51

Contrapunctus XIIa

There is also a second reshaping of the ground theme within Contrapunctus XIIa,b (Ex. 52). The antecedent phrase of this variation contains a number of tones which are interpolated between the pitches of the original ground theme (x), as well as a tie figure which is both approached and left by running sixteenth notes. This playful thematic reshaping actually foreshadows the coloratura

---

[9] [Translator's note: Because J.S. Bach personally supervised the publication of the first eleven contrapuncti, it is assumed that the published order of these contrapuncti was approved by the composer himself. But there has been much controversy about the correct ordering and numbering of the fugues (and canons) after Contrapunctus XI. For reasons stated in chapter 9, the author believes that the four-voice mirror-fugue pair should be labeled Contrapunctus XII. He will devote all of chapter 9 to a complete discussion of the numbering and ordering of the work's canons and fugues. Although he does not use the small case letters (a,b) after the Roman numerals to represent the individual fugues of the mirror pairs, this translation will employ them in an attempt to avoid as much confusion as possible.]

[10] It should be remembered that diatonic texture of Contrapunctus XIIa,b is in sharp contrast to the highly chromatic texture associated with Contrapunctus XI.

[11] Note the central position of the c♯ as it divides the subject into antecedent and consequent phrases.

variations of the ground theme which are found in the canons.[12] A highly stressed and ornamented discant-clausula figure (c#-d) is located at the midpoint of this variant. When inverted in Contrapunctus XIIb, the discant clausula figure changes to a similarly stressed pathopoetic returning-tone motive (a-b♭-a). The mirror imaging in this spot clearly prepares the way for the B-A-C-H-C#-D theme.[13]

EXAMPLE 52

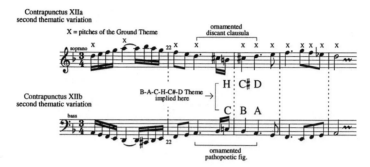

The brightest and most joyful moments of the entire work are found in Contrapunctus XIIIa,b. This three-voice mirror-fugue pair seems to make a rhetorical response to the message contained in Contrapunctus XIIa,b as early as the first subject entry (Ex. 53). Because of its opening octave leap,[14] and its giguelike triplet rhythm, the thematically reshaped subject of Contrapunctus XIIIa,b takes on a joyful dancelike character. This, in spite of the inserted dotted-note rhythm (Ex. 53, measure 4),[15] which is so widely employed in Contrapunctus II,

---

[12] [Translator's note: The author views the canons as somewhat auxiliary to the central thrust of *The Art of Fugue*. Nevertheless, he suggests the canons be placed after the second mirror-fugue pair (Contrapunctus XIIIa,b). See p.118.]

[13] [Translator's note: The subject of Contrapunctus XIIb was added on a separate staff beneath the subject of Contrapunctus XIIa. Ex. 52 has also been altered from the author's original. This addition was made so that the emergence of the B-A-C-H sphere in the mirroring process might be more clearly illustrated.]

[14] The octave leap at the beginning of Contrapunctus XIIIa,b is highly reminiscent of the octave leap which opens Contrapunctus IX. [Translator's note: Though the subject of Contrapunctus IX is often considered by analysts to be a "new" theme, the author will soon point out the hidden relationship that its subject maintains with both the normal and inverted forms of the ground theme (see p.106).]

[15] [Translator's note: The Berlin Autograph shows this dotted-note pattern in rhythmic diminution (dotted-sixteenth and thirty-second notes), as compared to the dotted-eighth and sixteenth-note patterns used in earlier contrapuncti. Though the rest of the notes in Eggebrecht's original Ex. 53 follow the Berlin autograph precisely, there are incorrectly notated dotted-eighth and sixteenth notes in measure 4. It is clear that these larger note values do not fit the meter signature; apparently a misprint. The rhythm of Example 53 has been corrected in this translation to match the Berlin Autograph.]

Contrapuncti V-VII, and Contrapunctus X. Although we previously associated these dotted-note rhythms with the affection of "stubborn willfulness," this affection is greatly tempered in Contrapunctus XIIIa,b by the surrounding triplet figures. Moreover, the actual pitch relationships of the dotted-note figures are also changed from the basic stepwise motion found in the earlier fugues, to joyfully leaping arpeggiated triads. These dotted-note arpeggiations are then carried over into the main body of Contrapunctus XIIIa,b, where they dominate the materials of the countervoices.

EXAMPLE 53

Contrapunctus XIIa: subject

Rhetorically, it is as if this dancelike pair of mirror fugues is responding with "joy" to the "act of mercy" established in Contrapunctus XIIa,b. In Contrapunctus XIIIa, the thematically reshaped subject enters first in inverted form, providing further evidence for this rhetorical interpretation.[16] Here, Bach's employment of thematic inversion can be understood to represent a human initiated reaction in response to the mercy of God.[17] Moreover, unlike the four-voice pair of mirror fugues, the mirroring in the three-voice pair is not as strictly developed.[18] It is entirely possible that the imperfect mirroring in Contrapunctus XIIIa,b could be symbolic of a human gesture that, though sincere, is less complete than the perfection of God's atoning mercy.

---

[16] [Translator's note: Modern published editions of *The Art of Fugue* by both Wolfgang Graeser (Breitkopf & Härtel) and Hermann Diener (Bärenreiter) follow the score placement found in Bach's Berlin Autograph (original [a], above; mirror inversion [b], below), whereas, the edition by Hans Gal (Boosey & Hawkes) states the two pairs of mirror fugues in a side-by-side fashion ([a] left; [b] right). In the first published edition of the work, however, the three-voice mirror pair (Contrapunctus XIII) is placed in what appears to be reversed order from that of the Berlin Autograph (entire [b] followed by entire [a]).]

[17] [Translator's note: That is, the subject of Contrapunctus XIIa is representative of an action initiated by God, whereas, the subject of Contrapunctus XIIIa is representative of the human response to this action—an inverse relationship.]

[18] [Translator's note: Whereas a four-voice texture may be symmetrically mirrored (the inversions of both the top and bottom, and the two middle staves exchanging places with each other), it is impossible to perfectly mirror a three-voice texture, since the voices must change positions in a non-symmetrical fashion.]

The Four Canons

The strongest examples of thematic variation are found in the work's four canons. Though these two-voice canons are not as texturally rich as the fugues, their lack of textural variety is somewhat counteracted by their great virtuosity and the abundance of their thematic variation.[19] The canons employed in *The Art of Fugue* are actually quite unique, since they attempt to approximate fugal form. Each canon begins by stating, in a single voice, a variation of the ground theme which is then immediately imitated by the second voice.[20] Even after the initial thematic statements and their contrapuntal imitations, however, these variations periodically return throughout the canons.[21] It should be noted, however, that Bach does not always confine these subsequent entries to the contrapuntal format in which they were initially stated. Later entries of the thematic variants may be found in tonal versions, inversion forms, or in other types of variation.[22] We shall limit our discussion to those thematic variants that appear at the opening of each of the four canons.

From the time of Bach's death to the present, there has been no way of determining exactly where in the cycle, and in what order, Bach intended to place the canons. It seems to me, however, that the most sensible solution in every respect is to group the canons together and let them stand as the penultimate section of the work. From time immemorial and in the widest variety of compositional forms, there has been a tendency for composers to place specially organized and highly ornamented musical structures in this next-to-last position. Enhancing the penultimate section, while providing contrast and variety near the end of a work, also adds additional weight and significance to the final section itself.[23]

As far as the specific ordering of the canons is concerned, I think that they should be arranged in ascending order of contrapuntal complexity, as determined by the pitch interval of imitation between the leader and the follower. Thus, the order: 1) canon at the octave; 2) canon at the twelfth; 3) canon at the tenth; and

---

[19] Unlike the two-voice canons (*fugæ ligatæ*), the fugues (*fugæ liberæ*) of the cycle are constructed in either three or four voices, and contain a number of textural differentiations produced by the alternation of entries and episodes.

[20] Analogous to the exposition of a fugue.

[21] Somewhat analogous to fugal alternation of post-expositional entries and episodes.

[22] Analogous to a tonal answer in fugue.

[23] [Translator's note: Placing the highly figured canons as a group in the penultimate position creates a textural change which functions like an extended and ornamented introduction to the closing fugue. In addition, this penultimate placement tends to set the closing fugue in relief, since the canons provide a dramatic change of genre from the preceding thirteen Contrapuncti.]

4) canon at the fourth below in augmented counter-motion. Both the manner of placement within the cycle and this suggested ordering of the four canons agree with the current opinion of most experts in the field.

Because the leader voice at the beginning tends to characterize each respective canon, we shall attempt to interpret the rhetorical meanings of these opening thematic variants.

The four canons are so lively and flexible that they are like miniature character studies on the human "I." Throughout the previous movements of the cycle, the human "I" has been slowly brought to an understanding of God's mercy. If the canons are actually placed in the penultimate position of the cycle, they seem to respond to the preceding "act of mercy" (mirror fugues) with a bright, lighthearted hope. To place the canons here also seems to provide additional rhetorical motivation for the closing fugue.[24]

The thematic variant in the first canon (Ex. 54) relates directly back to Contrapunctus XIIIa,b, because of its similarity to the inverted ground theme and its happy giguelike rhythm. The lighthearted character, which is maintained throughout, is further strengthened by joyful, chord-defining leaps found at the beginning of the countervoice [not shown in Ex. 54, see measure 5, soprano].

EXAMPLE 54

Canon alla Ottava

X = pitches of the inverted Ground Theme

In contrast to the bright playfulness of the first canon, the thematic variant which begins the second canon (Ex. 55) contains within it the elements of a drama in miniature. In this thematic variant, the human "I" must negotiate its way through a number of textural changes before its conflict is finally resolved. The variant begins with the same flowing sextuplet motion that was characteristic of the first canon, but this figure suddenly breaks off and the rhythm becomes slower (measures 2 and 3). The line then changes both direction and character (measure 4), and is brought to its midpoint by a downward diminished-seventh leap (measure 5). After the leap, the second half of the theme begins with a stepwise ascending approach to tonic followed by an energetic, sequencing motive. The goal pitches of each segment of this sequence are successively higher (measures 6-7). Though the basic motific pattern remains the same, the

---

[24] [Translator's note: It should be recalled that the author interprets the closing fugue as the place in the work where the human "I" is unified with God.]

rising sequence of the previous measures is now answered by a new sequence (measures 7-9), where the goal pitches of each segment drop successively lower until the final tonic pitch is reached.

EXAMPLE 55

Canon alla Duodecima in Contrapunto alla Quinta (circle canon)

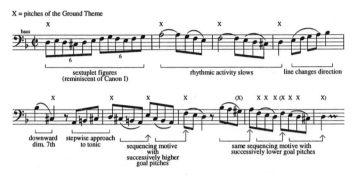

The ground-theme variant in the third canon (Ex. 56) is more obviously related to the inversion of the original ground theme. It is also characterized by constant syncopation, which continues throughout the movement, broken off only by a conspicuous quarter-note chromatic passage which descends through the interval of a perfect fourth (passus duriusculus).[25]

EXAMPLE 56

Canon alla Decima [in] Contrapunto alla Terza

syncopation of Ground-Theme materials (inverted form)

The thematic variant in the fourth canon (Ex. 57) picks up the mood suggested by the previous canon and greatly intensifies it. It contains both the combined rhetoric of exclamatio and pathopoeia in its opening figure (d-b♭-a), and the pathopoetic returning-tone figure (d-e♭-d). These chromatic variations, along with syncopation, "sighing" figures, stretto, and "false" intervals characterize the entire canon. In the fourth canon, both the musical materials and their respective rhetorical expressions refer back to Contrapunctus XI.

---

[25] [Translator's note: Passages containing passus duriusculus in the *Canon alla Decima* can be found in measures 19-20, bass; 23-24, soprano; 58-59, soprano; 62-63, bass.]

A further analogy can also be drawn between Contrapunctus XI and the final canon. In the same way that the chromatic character of Contrapunctus XI was immediately counteracted by the following mirror fugues, the chromatic "human frailty" of the fourth canon is also counteracted by the powerfully diatonic first section of the closing fugue. It is necessary only to compare the final printed version of this canon [with its intensified chromaticism and added slurs] to the Berlin Autograph to understand why it is best placed at the end of the cycle's penultimate group.[26]

EXAMPLE 57

Canon in Hypodiatessaron al roverscio e per augmentationem, perpetuus

Monothematicism in *The Art of Fugue*

The question of "new" themes in *The Art of Fugue* has already been tentatively answered: there are really no "new" themes in the cycle; that is, those several subjects in the work which do appear to be newly conceived should actually be regarded as melodic transformations of materials from the ground theme (thematic metamorphosis). We have already discussed both the rhetorical factors which appear to motivate the three closing fugue subjects and the methods by which these subjects were derived from specific segments of the ground theme. The first closing-fugue subject, which contains no half steps, was produced by reducing the ground theme to its most diatonic framework (p.13); the second closing-fugue subject, the "running theme," was derived from the thematic eighth-note figure at the end of the ground theme (p.21); and finally, the B-A-C-H-C♯-D theme was derived by combining the half-step motion that occurs in both the normal and inverted forms of the ground theme (p.11).

---

[26] [Translator's note: It should be pointed out that neither the Berlin Autograph nor the first published edition of *The Art of Fugue* places the *Canon in Hypodiatessaron al roverscio e per augmentationem, perpetuus* (Perpetual Canon at the Fourth Below in Augmented Counter-Motion) in the final position within the group of canons. The Berlin Autograph shows it third, and the first printed edition places it first. To compare the final printed version of this canon to the Berlin Autograph see: Johann Sebastian Bach, *Die Kunst der Fuge: from the autograph and the first print,* ed. Hermann Diener (Kassel, Bärenreiter Verlag) 1956: 137-43.]

In addition to the subjects of the closing fugue, however, there are also several other subjects which appear "new," but, in fact, are related to the ground theme by similar processes of thematic transformation. The very first of these other subjects is the step-leap subject which opens Contrapunctus VIII (Ex. 58b) This subject also serves as the second subject of Contrapunctus XI. We have already discussed how the step-leap subject, which descends more or less chromatically between two pitches a perfect fifth apart, was derived from the countersubject of Contrapunctus III (Ex. 40). As Example 58a,b shows, the three-note leaping motive of the step-leap subject is a melodic transformation of the opening motive of the suspiratio variation of the ground theme.

Though the first subject of Contrapunctus X is often considered a "new" subject, it also proves to be related to the three-note opening motive of the step-leap subject (Ex. 58b,c). Since the subject of Contrapunctus X opens with a mirrored three-note motive which is separated by an eighth rest, we shall call this ground theme transformation the *rest-mirror* subject.

EXAMPLE 58

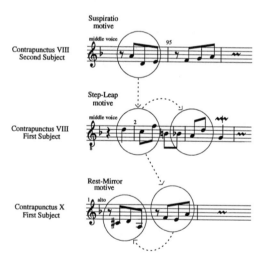

The relationship between the suspiratio variation and the three-note leaping motive of the step-leap subject (Ex. 58a,b) is particularly clear in a passage beginning on the anacrusis note to measure 80 of Contrapunctus VIII (Ex. 59). Here in the soprano, two suspiratio motives directly precede a complete entry of the step-leap subject. Notice that these two suspiratio motives are also set in counterpoint against a false entry of the step-leap subject in the alto.

EXAMPLE 59

Contrapunctus VII

Of all of the so-called "new" themes in *The Art of Fugue,* only the first subject of Contrapunctus IX remains to be discussed (Ex. 60). We shall refer to this subject as the *joyful octave-leap* theme since it seems to embody a clear, light, and peaceful character. Contrapunctus IX is the second of the group of four fugues on multiple subjects and it is placed directly before the silent symmetrical axis of the cycle (more about this in chapter 9). In fact, the method by which this fugue closes off the first symmetrical part of the cycle foreshadows the way in which the complete work will end; that is, with one subject acting like the countersubject to another. From measure 18 on, the first subject of Contrapunctus IX functions like a countersubject to the ground theme, which appears here in unaltered form for the first time since Contrapunctus I.

The subject of Contrapunctus IX also has a direct relationship to the ground theme, however. In the same way that the B-A-C-H-C#-D theme was formed by juxtaposing elements of the ground theme's inverted and normal forms, the first subject of Contrapunctus IX also takes its shape from elements of both forms of the ground theme (Ex. 60).

EXAMPLE 60

Contrapunctus IX: first subject

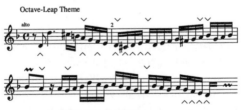

∧ = pitches from normal form of the Ground Theme
∨ = pitches from inverted form of the Ground Theme

Though it is likely that the episodic and accompanimental materials of the cycle may also be further variations or metamorphoses of the ground theme, I must concede that it is not absolutely certain. I shall leave this for the reader to investigate further. In any such study, however, it will not always be possible to know if connections between particular musical materials of the cycle and the ground theme were established intentionally or accidentally. The structure of the ground theme is too elementary to allow for any conclusive proof.

9

The Cycle

Ⓘ f Bach's *The Art of Fugue* is to be adequately appraised as a complete cycle, we must first clearly establish the order of its movements. The question of this order has been intensely debated, however, and has resulted in much disagreement. It is not my intention to cover the collected research in this area completely or to discuss all of the problems associated with the traditions surrounding the work. However, since my arguments about the order of the movements and the rhetorical content which determines that order are dependent upon current scholarly research, I must refer to those studies which are crucial to the premises of this book. To begin, it is essential that we examine the well-documented, two-step origin of *The Art of Fugue.*

The appearance of Bach's autograph manuscript (Berlin Autograph) is the first known document in the evolution of the work. The manuscript is a fair copy which is notated in full score. The individual movements are tightly placed one after the other and numbered with Roman numerals from I-XV. Though the fugues are not titled (either as *Fuga* or *Contrapunctus),* the two canons contained in the manuscript are labeled *Canon.* After analyzing the handwriting and the paper used in this manuscript, Christoph Wolff claims that Bach finished a considerable portion (at least two-thirds) of this fair copy by the early 1740's, and concludes that Bach actually started work on *The Art of Fugue,* not in the late 1740's, but rather in the late 1730's.[1] The complete contents of the Berlin Autograph are listed in Table 1.

It will never be known with absolute certainty whether Bach considered this fair copy to be merely a preliminary and somewhat arbitrary collection of fugues based on the ground theme, or whether he considered it to be an embryonic

---

[1] Christoph Wolff, "Zur Chronologie und Kompositionsgeschichte von Bachs 'Kunst der Fuge'," *Beitrag zur Musikwissenschaft* (1983): 130-42.

TABLE 1

Contents of the Berlin Autograph

I	Simple Fugue	4	Normal	Tied-note Figures
II	Simple Fugue	4	Inverted	Chromaticism
III	Simple Fugue	4	Normal	Dotted-note Rhythm; Final Cadence on A-major
IV	Counterfugue	4	Normal + Inverted (dotted -note fig.)	Subject found in only one durational format (no augmentation or diminution)
V	Double Fugue	4	"Octave-Leap Theme" + Normal	
VI	Double Fugue	4	Inverted (dotted-note fig.)+ "Rest-Mirror Theme"	
VII	Counterfugue	4	Normal + Inverted (both with dotted-note fig.)	Subject found in two durational formats (standard and diminution)
VIII	Counterfugue	4	Normal + Inverted (both with dotted-note fig.)	Subject found in three durational formats (standard, diminution, and augmentation)
IX	Canon in Hypodiapason	2		Notated first as a single voice, followed immediately by a complete two-voice realization
X	Double Fugue with single countersubject ("Triple Fugue")	3	"Walk-Leap Theme" + Inverted (rests) + Countersubject in stretto	
XI	Double Fugue with two countersubjects ("Triple/Quadru-ple Fugue")	4	Normal + Inverted (with rests) + "Walk-Leap Theme" + Chromatic Countersubject + Countersubject in Stretto	
XII	Canon in Augmentation	2		Notated first in complete two-voice realization, followed by single-voice version (Canon in Hypodiatessaron al roverscio e per augmentationem, perpetuus)
XIII	Mirror Fugue	4	Normal + Inverted; 3/4 meter	Initial form (normal form of subject) notated on upper score; mirror-image form (inverted subject) notated on lower score
XIV	Mirror Fugue	3	Normal/Inverted; 16th-note triplets	Initial form (inverted subject) notated on upper score; mirror-image form (normal form of subject) notated on lower score
XV	Canon al roverscio et per augmentationem	2		Notated in two-voice format; an arrangement of XII (contains same melody as XII)

design which guided the production of a more fully conceived final version. A somewhat valid case can be made for the latter, since the order of the movements in the Berlin Autograph points toward the order of the final version in the following ways:

1) The forms, materials and techniques of the Berlin Autograph progress systematically from one movement to the next. The manuscript begins with the simple fugues, then moves on progressively to counter- and double fugues, double fugues with countersubjects, and finally, to the mirror fugues. At the same time, the contrapuntal techniques employed in the Berlin Autograph also progress from simpler devices to those that are more complex: Nos. I-III, simple (noninvertible) counterpoint; Nos. IV-IX, double-invertible counterpoint with various intervals of inversion, along with the appearance of diminution and augmentation; Nos. X and XI, triple-invertible counterpoint; and Nos. XIII and XIV, mirroring in both simple and double-invertible counterpoint.

2) The various fugal types are placed together in groups, and these groups seem to be symmetrically arranged. In the group of simple fugues, Nos. I and III, which are based on the normal (noninverted) form of the ground theme, provide a symmetrical frame for No. II, which is based on the inversion of the ground theme. Moreover, Number III ends on the dominant (A-major triad) in preparation for a return to tonic at the beginning of the next group. In the second group, the first two of the three counterfugues (Nos. IV, VII) act as framing movements for the two double fugues (Nos. V and VI). Perhaps Bach arranged the fugues of the second group in this order since the normal and inverted forms of the ground theme appear in opposition to each other in Nos. IV and VII, and Nos. V and VI. The third counterfugue (No. VIII) might have been deliberately isolated from the symmetry of the second group so that it could stand alone as the axis of symmetry for the entire manuscript.

3) Though somewhat separated from each other (by the symmetrical considerations discussed in 2), the three counterfugues do show increasing complexity. Whereas the two subjects of No. IV do not contain entries in augmentation or diminution, the subjects in No. VII occur in both standard durational format and in diminution; the subjects in No. VIII are found in standard format, diminution and augmentation.

4) It is more difficult to provide symmetrical groupings for Nos. IX-XV. Perhaps the two canons (Nos. IX and XII) could be considered framing movements for the two "triple fugues" (Nos. X and XI), thereby providing an appropriate four-movement balance to the group of counter and double fugues (Nos. IV-VII), but this would leave the two mirror fugues at the end (Nos. XIII and XIV) without a symmetrical counterpart at the beginning of the manuscript (two mirror fugues vs. three simple fugues). If the canons (Nos. IX and XII) are considered only as free articulation points in the structure, however, No. VIII then loses its position as the central axis of symmetry.

Until now, the final canon of the manuscript (No. XV) has almost always been considered just an arrangement of No. XII, pointing ahead [as though it were simply an appended movement to the Berlin Autograph] to a more fully conceived version of the work. Since No. XV shares its melody with No. XII (the realization is quite different, however), it is possible that No. XV should be considered a separate movement with enough weight to adequately counterbalance No. XII. In this case, the augmentation canon No. XII could function as a major articulation of symmetry in the complete structure, while also providing (with No. XV) a bordering framework for the two mirror fugues.

In spite of the possibilities discussed in the preceding five points, much of this remains sheer speculation. Although there is recognizable intentional symmetry in the first and second groups of the manuscript, No. VIII is not independent enough in character to function as a true central axis, and the canons carry far less weight than the surrounding "triple" and mirror fugues. Though the canons can certainly be considered points of articulation, their lack of weight and their position in the order completely counteracts an interpretation of the form based on a central axis of symmetry.

To a certain extent, the order of the fugues and canons in the Berlin Autograph also agrees with our rhetorical interpretation of the work. In this early manuscript, however, the rhetorical change of character between "human frailty" and "mercy" is most clearly evident between the highly chromatic "triple fugues" (Nos. X and XI) and the following mirror fugues (Nos. XII and XIV). The only movement in this manuscript version capable of bringing the work to a conclusion (according to our interpretation), would be the dancelike three-voice mirror fugue (No. XIV). The canon, No. XV, with its pathopoetic, chromatic character, reintroduces elements of "human frailty" and therefore cannot function as a closing movement.

The Berlin Autograph seems to be a temporary stage in the development of *The Art of Fugue,* in which certain aspects of the work's more definitive later appearing form are represented. Though only tentative in the Berlin Autograph, certain features such as the placing of the movements into groups, the symmetrical nature of the groups, the construction of the work around a central axis, and the presence of rhetorical content foreshadow the later version.

It is quite possible that Bach wrote out the Berlin Autograph directly after one of his early work sessions in order to take inventory of the work and place all of the completed movements together. It is also possible that he produced the manuscript before a later work session, perhaps after a period of many interruptions. In any case, the Berlin Autograph can be considered a model of certain goals and directions for the work which were not yet in definitive form.

Important, although also unanswerable, is the question of when Bach first conceived the idea to finish the cycle with a quadruple fugue, whose last "new" subject would be the B-A-C-H-C#-D theme. It is possible that Bach realized this potential only after the Berlin Autograph was completed. If this were the case, the ideas of a ground theme, the B-A-C-H sphere, and the B-A-C-H motto itself probably would not have been planned from the very beginning. Instead these materials would have crystallized, more or less accidentally, from the opening d-minor gesture out of which all the ideas in the cycle can be derived.

Since the quadruple fugue is the "crowning jewel" of *The Art of Fugue,* I cannot imagine that Bach did not carry with him any thoughts about this final movement from before the time of the Berlin Autograph. Furthermore, he must have conceived some basic outline of the last movement from the very inception of the work, especially the ideas of returning again to the ground theme, the use of the B-A-C-H theme, and the employment of mirror-fugue technique. In the same way that it tentatively sets forth groups of movements, progressions of compositional techniques, and the concept of axial symmetry (hallmarks of the final version of the cycle), the Berlin Autograph also sets forth a tentative rhetorical statement about the relationship between the "nature of God" *(Sein)* and "human nature" *(Dasein).* This rhetorical statement is only perfected later, however, with the entry of the B-A-C-H-C♯-D theme in the last contrapunctus of the final version.

Though an embryonic representation of rhetorical meaning is evident in the Berlin Autograph, it becomes much more fully developed and clearly worked out in the later version, especially as the closing fugue begins to take on concrete shape and form. Therefore, on the levels of materials and techniques as well as rhetorical content, there exists a relationship between the prototype Berlin Autograph and the later final version of the work. In short, the Berlin Autograph is to the final version of *The Art of Fugue* as "initial insight" is to "mature concept."

We shall now discuss the errors that found their way into the first printing of the work after the death of the composer.

Wolfgang Wiemer has established with great certainty that the process of engraving the plates for *The Art of Fugue* began sometime in the year 1748.[2] Wiemer also claimed, however, that the order of Contrapuncti I-XIII was firmly established at the time of Bach's death. I intend to dispute this latter statement, since there is little doubt that the order of the normal and inverted forms of the two mirror fugues should be exchanged from the way they appear in the first printed edition.

In the first publication, the double fugue (No. VI in the Berlin Autograph) follows the two mirror fugues. Apparently it was not noticed that this entire fugue, with the addition of a newly composed and appended beginning section of eleven measures ("portal"),[3] had already been employed in the cycle as

---

[2] Wolfgang Wiemer, "Zur Datierung des Erstdrucks der 'Kunst der Fuge'," *Musikforschung* 31 (1978): 181-85.

[3] [Translator's note: The author will shortly explain his use of the term *portal* in the sections dealing with the work's central axis and the "mirror-rest" theme.]

Contrapunctus X. This error (and I cannot emphasize this point strongly enough) strikes full in the face the concept of grouping, movement progression, and symmetry. Moreover, it completely silences the rhetorical intention of the cycle. Evidently Carl Philipp Emanuel and Bach's student, Johann Friedrich Agricola, did not fully understand the nature of *The Art of Fugue,* since they were the ones who must have been responsible for this and other errors that appear in the first printed edition.

The order of the canons in the first edition (augmentation, octave, third, fifth) does not agree with Bach's basic approach to the work. Though this conclusion does not agree with Wiemer, all aspects of his study, as was indicated above, may not be totally reliable. My view on the correct ordering of the canons (octave, fifth, third, augmentation) was discussed in chapter 8.

In the first printed edition, a two-keyboard, four-voice arrangement of the three-voice mirror fugue is inserted between the canons and the closing fugue. As opposed to the almost universally held view that the three-voice mirror fugue was written to be played on a pedal harpsichord, Werner Breig convincingly argues that this mirror fugue is, instead, primarily a demonstration of pure contrapuntal technique.[4] Furthermore, Breig holds that Bach probably created the two-keyboard arrangement, which includes a fourth "free" (unmirrored) contrapuntal voice, in order to make the materials of this fugue more idiomatic for keyboard players. According to Breig, the two-keyboard arrangement should actually be considered parenthetical to *The Art of Fugue,* and would be best included in an appendix to the work. This interpretation, insofar as it is correct, confirms the notion that Bach's primary purpose for the cycle was the demonstration of pure contrapuntal art, rather than the production of idiomatically performable pieces.

Since we have already addressed the problem of attaching the organ chorale *(Wenn wir in höchsten Nöten sein)* to the end of the first published edition (chapter 4), it will require no further comment here. Moreover, since the first printed edition of *The Art of Fugue* likely contains errors in the order of the movements, I refer the reader to Table 2, where I have suggested an alternative that seems to better agree with both the structure and rhetoric of the work.

As opposed to the contents of the Berlin Autograph, the motivation behind Bach's addition of materials and change of movement order in the first publication is quite clear. The contrapuncti are now all arranged in groups according to fugal type. In addition, they are also ordered, one after the other, in an ever increasing level of contrapuntal complexity. Moreover, the first published edition contains two more canons than were found in the Berlin Autograph, and the group of canons is now placed in the penultimate position of the work.

---

4 Werner Breig, "Bachs 'Kunst der Fuge': Zur instrumentalen Bestimmung und zum Zyklus-Charakter," *Bach-Jahrbuch* (1982): 103-23.

Table 2

Suggested Disposition of Movements in *The Art of Fugue*

I	I	Simple Fugue	4	Normal	Tied-note Figures
II	III	Simple Fugue	4	Normal	Dotted-note Rhythm
III	II	Simple Fugue	4	Inverted	Chromaticism
IV	-	Simple Fugue	4	Inverted	Leaps in Thirds
V	IV	Counterfugue	4	Inverted + Normal (both with dotted notes)	Subject appears in one durational format (no. dim. or aug.)
VI	VII	Counterfugue	4	Normal + Inverted (both with dotted notes)	Subject appears in two durational formats (std. and dim.)
VII	VIII	Counterfugue	4	Normal + Inverted (both with dotted notes)	Subject appears in three durational formats (std., dim., and aug.)
VIII	X	Double Fugue with one countersubject ("Triple Fugue")	3	"Walk-leap Theme" + Inverted (rests) + countersubject in stretto	
IX	V	Double Fugue	4	"Octave-leap Theme" + Normal	
X	[VI]	Double Fugue	4	Inverted (dotted notes) + "Rest-mirror Theme"	
XI	XI	Double Fugue with two countersubjects ("Triple/Quadruple Fugue")	4	Normal/Inverted (rests) + "Walk-leap Theme" + chromatic countersubject + countersubject in stretto	
XII [a,b]	XIII	Mirror Fugue	4	Normal/Inverted; 3/4 meter	Initial form [a] (normal subject) Mirror form [b] (inverted subject)
XIII [a,b]	XIV	Mirror Fugue	4	Inverted/Normal 16th-note triplets	Initial form [a] (inverted subject) Mirror form [b] (normal subject)
-	IX	Canon	2		At the 8ve
-	-	Canon	2		At the 12th in counterpoint at the 5th
-	-	Canon	2		At the 10th in counterpoint at the 3rd
-	XV	Canon	2		By augmentation in contrary motion
XIV	-	Quadruple Fugue (fragment)	4	"Reduction Theme" + Running theme" + "B-A-C-H Theme" + Ground Theme	
Appendix	-	Alternate version of XIII	4		For two harpsichords (extra voice added)

In the first published edition, the group of simple fugues is expanded by one additional movement (Contrapunctus IV is newly added). This is probably so that the first group (simple fugues) can act as a symmetrical counterbalance to the [planned] quadruple fugue at the end of the work. Inside the first group itself, the first and second fugues employ the normal form of the ground theme, while the third and fourth employ the inversion of the ground theme (N-N-I-I).[5] The endings of the three simple fugues in the Berlin Autograph are all changed in the first publication. As we discussed in chapter 5 (p.47), an extra four measures, containing one final entry of the subject, are added to the coda of Berlin Autograph No. I to enhance the dramatic rising of tessitura at its end.

Berlin Autograph No. II is provided with six additional measures of coda in the first published edition (Contrapunctus III). This expanded coda also contains an additional entry of the subject (see Contrapunctus III: 79-84, soprano), which was probably added so that the fugue could cadence on tonic harmony, like all the other fugues of the cycle.[6] Similarly, Berlin Autograph No. III is fitted with an extra two measures of coda (see Contrapunctus II: 70-72), perhaps so that the soprano might resolve to the root of the tonic chord [perfect authentic cadence] in the final version, rather than to the third.

As opposed to the successive presentation of the normal and inverted forms of the ground theme in the first group, each of the counterfugues in the second group employs both normal and inverted forms of the ground theme. This group of counterfugues, with its reliance on thematic inversion, provides a symmetrical counterbalance to the mirror-fugue group in the second half of the work.[7]

The third group, which forms the central axis of the entire cycle, contains four fugues on multiple subjects. Moreover, the individual fugues which make up this group are arranged so that the group itself is symmetrically ordered [double fugue + one countersubject; double fugue; double fugue; double fugue + two countersubjects]. It is between the two, four-voice double fugues (Contrapuncti IX and X) that the "silent" axis of the entire work occurs. After this "silent" axis, the symmetrical "replay" of both the group and the complete cycle begins. I interpret the materials which Bach appended to the Berlin Autograph No.VI, and which now appear at the start of Contrapunctus X, as the

---

5 [Translator's note: It should be remembered that Berlin Autograph Nos. II and III exchange places in the first published edition to become Contrapunctus III and II, respectively.]

6 [Translator's note: The final cadence chord of Berlin Autograph No. II is an A-major chord (dominant of D-minor). It should be noted that this is the only time in the primary source documents belonging to *The Art of Fugue* where a movement of the cycle ends on harmony other than tonic.]

7 [Translator's note: Note that the counterfugue group not only symmetrically counterbalances the mirror-fugue group, but that the presence of thematic (subject) inversion in the counterfugues also foreshadows the more sophisticated techniques of total inversion employed in the mirror fugues.]

"portal" through which we are ushered into the second half of the symmetrical structure in *The Art of Fugue*.

Contrapunctus X begins with the rest-mirror subject (Ex. 61), which is derived from the suspiratio form of the ground theme (Ex. 58). The "sighing" three-note motive at the opening of the "portal" is, after an intervening rest, followed by another three-note figure which is an intervallic mirror image of the opening motive. Furthermore, though not perfectly symmetrical, the upward and downward passage of sixteenth notes (measure 2, alto) which follows these opening mirror motives also strongly implies a sense of mirror-image construction. The concept of large formal inversion is also symbolized in the materials of the "portal" by the entries of the inverted form of the rest-mirror theme (measure 3, bass) and the stretto entries of both its normal and inverted forms (measures 7-8; alto, tenor).

EXAMPLE 61

Contrapunctus X: rest-mirror theme (beginning of the "portal" addition)

Because of the nature of this added "portal" material, Contrapunctus X is the only fugue in the cycle which does not begin on either the tonic pitch d or the dominant pitch a. Instead, this double fugue begins on the leading tone c♯, which, perhaps, also symbolizes its position in the center of the work (directly after the "silent" axis), in the same way that c♯ forms the central turning point of the ground theme.

The form of the complete work can be seen as an enlarged projection of the symmetry and pitch progression which characterize the ground theme. Analogous to the way that the materials of this thematic source proceed from and return to the pitch d, the overall structure of the work was planned to begin and end with the unaltered ground theme. In addition, the manner in which it progresses from its beginning to its midpoint and from its midpoint to its end corresponds, respectively, to the function of the counterfugue and mirror-fugue groups in the overall form.

The central group of four fugues (Contrapuncti VIII-XI) is also a powerful projection of the midpoint of the ground theme. The pitches d-c♯-d from the center of the ground theme and the pitches a-b♭-a from the center of the inverted ground theme generate both the diminished-seventh chord and all other chromatic expression in the work. Further, it is out of these basic chromatic gestures that the B-A-C-H-C#-D sphere is formed. In our interpretation, the half-step returning-tone motive (and the chromaticism it initiates) represents the essence of the "human condition" (*Dasein*). Since the group of fugues in the center of *The Art of Fugue* contain the most highly chromatic materials in the work (thereby raising the rhetorical statement about the "human condition" to its zenith), it is possible to draw an analogy between the half-step returning-tone motive at the center of the ground theme and this group of highly chromatic fugues in the center of the work.

We shall now briefly discuss the four fugues of the central group. In the process, we will also employ those names, coined earlier, that help describe the character and rhetorical content of their subjects.

The first double fugue (Contrapunctus VIII) begins with the step-leap theme. This ground-theme variant contains both the pitches of the B-A-C-H sphere as well as direct stepwise chromatic motion. Here, the step-leap theme is contrapuntally accompanied by a quasi-chromatic countersubject (measures 39-42, alto).[8] This same countersubject, which also appears later in stretto, connects the step-leap theme to the second subject (measures 152-57).[9] The second subject, which is actually the inversion form of the suspiratio theme, first appears in measure 94 (alto).

The second double fugue (Contrapunctus IX) is characterized by the joyful octave-leap theme. From its position in front of the "silent" axis of the work, this movement foreshadows the employment of the unaltered ground theme which was to have completed the work in the closing fugue. In fact, outside of the first fugal group and the [planned, but not completed, entry at the end of the] closing fugue, this is the only other movement in which the unaltered ground theme appears at all.

The third double fugue (Contrapunctus X), whose eleven measure "portal" introduces the second half of the symmetry in the work, joins together the suspiratio figure found in the rest-mirror theme with the "willful desire" motive which occurs in the dotted-note variant of the ground theme.

The final fugue in this group (Contrapunctus XI) is connected, in both materials and rhetorical content, to the three-voice double fugue (Contrapunctus VIII). Chromatic expression in the cycle is brought to its point of highest

---

8 [Translator's note: It is important to remember that the author considers this subjectlike, quasi-chromatic passage to be countersubject material in Contrapunctus VIII. Though it is not introduced in the initial exposition, once it does enter, this melodic material recurs so regularly (though the initial motive is often changed from a tied quarter- and eighth-note figure to three eighth notes) that it is considered by many analysts to be the second subject of a "triple" fugue.]

9 [Translator's note: The first stretto appearance of the countersubject occurs between the bass and the alto (measure 81), where the alto voice enters over the end of the bass statement. After this point, however, the countersubject is found in a number of different stretto configurations.]

intensity here in this final double fugue. The expressive intention of Contrapunctus XI is made clear by the presence of the suspiratio theme, the quasi-chromatic countersubject, the pitches of the B-A-C-H motto, "sighing" suspension figures, syncopation, and strong dissonances.

The final movement of each group in the work also provides a climax for the group. Contrapunctus IV, which ends the group of simple fugues and whose symmetrical position corresponds to the first section of the closing fugue, establishes an uplifting affection of joy. The augmented form of the "willful" dotted-note variant in Contrapunctus VII gives the impression of a free cantus firmus whose successive entries rise from the bass to the soprano. In the process of chromatic climax, Contrapunctus XI brings the rhetorical expression of the "human condition" and the "I am" (Bach) to its greatest intensity in *The Art of Fugue*. The lighthearted sixteenth-note triplet motion of the second mirror fugue (Contrapunctus XIIIa,b) is a joyful reaction to the rhetorical symbolism of "mercy" present in the mirroring process. The final canon returns us temporarily again to chromatic space before the entry of the closing fugue. Similarly, we have shown that the fourth and last section of the closing fugue would have been the goal and high point of the entire work (had Bach lived to actually complete it).[10]

Although it is possible to see, play, and hear the relationships above, there is no way to certify that our conclusions about the meanings of these relationships are correct, even though it is through study of these relationships that we have been able to establish our interpretation of the B-A-C-H motto. Though the B-A-C-H motto is always potentially present in the background of the musical materials in *The Art of Fugue,* it is most clearly perceptible in three places. The first of these spots is found in the coda of the last simple fugue (Contrapunctus IV).[11] Though it is dispersed between two voices (alto and tenor), the B-A-C-H motto in this joyful fugue is based on a partitioning of the complete B-A-C-H-C♯-D theme (Ex.21). The second spot occurs at the beginning of part two in Contrapunctus XI. This time, a straightforward and unaltered B-A-C-H motive (alto) becomes completely absorbed into the rhetorical content of the "human condition" (Ex. 43). Finally, the B-A-C-H motto appears, in its complete thematic (subject) form, in part three of the closing fugue. It is this appearance of the motto that was the starting point for our interpretation of the entire work.

---

[10] [Translator's note: Since the major premise of this book depends on the view that Bach planned to unite the ground theme with the closing fugue's first two subjects and the B-A-C-H-C♯-D theme in the fourth and final section of the fugue, the author considers this last section to be both the rhetorical goal of the entire work as well as the climax of the closing fugue.]

[11] It should be recalled, that Contrapunctus IV is not found in the Berlin Autograph, but does appear in the first published edition of *The Art of Fugue.*

10

Assimilation into the Repertoire

Historical Overview

The scope of this book will neither allow me to adequately interpret the cultural impact of *The Art of Fugue* and its assimilation into the repertoire, nor to cover in depth the many ways it has been viewed and evaluated. I shall provide a brief overview of these subjects, however, and introduce one additional topic that is of particular importance to me—the question of public performance.

Sales of *The Art of Fugue* were very modest in the years immediately after it first became available in print. This practically insured that the essence of Bach's artistry, particularly those basic principles of structural organization which should have been clearly recognizable, would be overlooked or misunderstood. Moreover, the immediate post-Bach generation often studied only isolated musical elements in the work, rather than considering the broader aspects of its organizational system; that is, they did not generally view *The Art of Fugue* in terms of those musical interrelationships which connect compositional goals and processes to principles of counterpoint, practical considerations to theoretical ideals, or musical form to rhetorical content.

The new generation, with its changing stylistic tastes, apparently did not recognize the wider-ranging implications present in the musical materials, rejected out-of-hand the concept of this kind of compositional organization, or completely misunderstood the manner in which the musical interrelationships should have been interpreted. Even those musicians who were best acquainted with the work proved to be quite unaware of its vast network of musical ideas. Instead, the post-Bach generation chose to focus its attention on individual details at the expense of a more comprehensive view.

Evidence of a change in approach to composition even appears in the foreword to the first printed edition of the work. Written by the Berlin theorist Friedrich Wilhelm Marpurg, it was probably added to the printed score at the request of Carl Philipp Emanuel Bach, so that *The Art of Fugue* might be brought to wider public attention by way of a respected musical authority.[1] This foreword, however, contains no mention of performance considerations.[2]

Marpurg asserts that Bach's method of composition exemplifies "the deepest study and practice of harmony," and that Bach had "never been surpassed" in this regard. Marpurg then goes on to comment on the state of contemporary composition by comparing, though in a somewhat overly partisan fashion, the differences between Bach and the younger generation of composers. He compares the master's polished compositional craft with "today's rubbish of effeminate *(weibliche)* song" and with "the skipping, superficial melodies *(Melodienmacherey)* of so many contemporary composers." He also attempts to convince the reader that Bach's melodic writing was both deeply conceived and "natural." He affirms that Bach always maintained the highest level of musical "taste" and, therefore, the composer's work merits "universal acclaim." In attempting to equate the music of Bach with "taste," however, Marpurg actually appeals to the aesthetic sensibilities of the younger generation. Indeed, the term "natural" was a fashionable analytical buzzword of the immediate post-Bach era.

Marpurg argues that Bach reconciles, "in the fugues and contrapuncti" of this work, "the rules of fugue" [with the compositional process] so that they may be suitably adapted to the needs of every composer. In the midst of this argument, however, Marpurg mentions the widely held view that "fugue was born in antique absurdity." Furthermore, he states that the term *counterpoint* is considered by "the tender ears of our present time . . . [to be of value for little more than the production of] . . . barbaric sounds." By reference to such views, Marpurg confirms that his contemporaries actually considered counterpoint and composition as separate entities. He even discusses this issue in such a way that the separation between the two appears to be self-evident. Implying this separation between counterpoint and composition, and calling attention to the "antiquated" nature of fugue, Marpurg underscores the notion that *The Art of Fugue* is little more than a pedagogical treatise. "In earlier times," he continues, "fugue was considered to be the most magnificent and ornamented music of both sacred and secular genres, and indeed, one still comes across a fugue now and then in the former category, although it has taken its final farewell from the latter."

From the time of the first printing of *The Art of Fugue* until autumn of 1756 only about thirty copies were sold. This figure was reported by C.P.E. Bach in a notice of September 14, 1756 in which he sought a publisher who was willing

---

[1] See *Vorbericht* (Foreword) in the facsimile of the first printed version; Johann Sebastian Bach, *Die Kunst der Fuge (BWV 1080): Autograph and Originaldruck,* (Leipzig: VEB Deutscher Verlag für Musik, 1979), title page overleaf.

[2] Marpurg signed and dated this foreword, *"in der Leipziger Ostermeße,* 1752" (Eastertide, Leipzig 1752).

to risk printing and distributing the work, as well as actively promoting its sales.[3] The reasons for such miserable sales of the first edition unfortunately remain lost in obscurity. From this point to the end of the notice, C.P.E. extols the work as "the most complete and practical fugal work." He goes on to say that *The Art of Fugue* would make an excellent supplement to "a good theory text, such as Marpurg's,[4] and, with the aid of these materials, a student could actually acquire good fugue-writing skills without having to pay great sums to learn the secrets of fugue from a master teacher."

It was a tragedy that Bach's final work, at the time of its first introduction to the public, was regarded as little more than a practical handbook or a collection of pedagogical examples for a topic that hardly anyone wanted to study. This initial lack of interest in *The Art of Fugue* was to take a dramatic turn for the better in the nineteenth century, but, even then, comprehension of the cycle was to be somewhat tentative, and limited primarily to individual movements and to a few of its many perceivable levels.

A gradual revival of interest in the works of Bach in the late-eighteenth and nineteenth centuries provided an important impetus for fresh examination of *The Art of Fugue*.[5] In fact, one of the earliest known examples of rekindled interest in the cycle is found in the contrapuntal studies of Wolfgang Amadeus Mozart. In his *Arrangement of Five Bach Fugues for String Trio* (K.V. 404a), Mozart places an arrangement of Contrapunctus VIII from *The Art of Fugue* directly after an arrangement of the *Adagio e dolce* from Bach's *Third Organ Sonata*. It is quite certain that these trio arrangements, like the five additional fugue settings from Bach's *Well-Tempered Clavier* Mozart arranged for string quartet (K.V. 405), were transcribed for the Sunday musical matinees that began taking place in the early 1780s at the home of Baron van Swieten in Vienna. Mozart wrote to his father on April 10, 1782: "Every Sunday about noon, I go to Baron van Swieten's, where nothing is played other than Handel and Bach. . . . I am in the process of making a collection of Bach fugues, Sebastian, as well as Emanuel and Friedemann Bach."

Further evidence that there was at least some practical interest in Bach's *The Art of Fugue* during this period is found in rehearsal books belonging to the orchestra school attached to the Berlin Singing Academy. These record books, dating from 1813-1815, indicate that individual contrapuncti from the cycle

---

3 At that time, C.P.E. had the engraved copper plates of *The Art of Fugue* in his possession.

4 C.P.E. refers here to Friedrich Wilhelm Marpurg's two volume treatise, *Abhandlung von der Fuge*, Berlin, 1753-54.

5 An important source of information for this historical discussion is found in: Walter Kolneder, *Kunst der Fuge. Mythen des 20. Jahrhunderts* (Wilhelmshaven: Taschenbücher zur Musikwissenschaft, Band IV, no. 45, 1977).

were occasionally rehearsed, but nothing is known about any subsequent public performances.

Mozart's interest in the pedagogical nature of *The Art of Fugue* was also shared by a number of nineteenth-century composers, such as Beethoven, Schumann, Bruckner and Brahms. This interest was probably due to the fact that *The Art of Fugue,* more than any other work, offers direct insight into Bach's harmonic procedures, contrapuntal techniques, and methods of fugal composition. Ludwig van Beethoven's estate contained both a hand-copied manuscript (not in Beethoven's hand) as well as a printed edition of the work (probably by Nägli); Schumann produced his own keyboard reduction (1837), while Anton Bruckner completed his own hand copy as a seventeen-year-old (1840-1841). Johannes Brahms acquired a copy of the manuscript in 1845.

A version of *The Art of Fugue* was published by Vogt (Paris 1801).[6] This was soon followed by Hans Georg Nägeli's edition (Zürich 1802), in which a two-stave keyboard reduction appeared below open-score notation. Nägli's edition was published as volume two in his series *Musikalische Kunstwerke im Strengen Style von J.S. Bach und anderen Meistern (Musical Artworks in Strict Style by J.S. Bach and other Masters).* Nägli was probably moved to produce this edition because there was an increasing public interest in Bach's "strict style," and a burgeoning demand for piano literature. This edition was also later reprinted in the mid-1820s by Richault (Paris).

In 1838, C.F. Peters (Leipzig) published *The Art of Fugue* as volume three of a large-scale edition of Bach works. This publication, in two-stave piano format, was edited by Carl Czerny, who provided fingerings, tempo markings, and other editorial observations. In a notice from the publisher, however, it was later admitted that "after several years in music stores, *The Art of Fugue* had completely failed," despite the fact that the primary intention of the edition was to make it easier to study and play the work at the keyboard. Kolneder established that approximately 2,700 copies of *The Art of Fugue* were sold from the time of its first printing until 1874.[7] He further determined that about 20,300 copies were sold up to 1926, because of the constant increase in new editions and the reprinting of older versions.

After 1838, Bach's *The Art of Fugue* was continuously available in practical [two-stave] piano editions. In 1868, the Leipzig firm of Reiter-Biedermann published an edition for organ, and the year 1875 saw publication of *The Art of Fugue* as volume twenty-five of *The Collected Works of Bach (Bach Gesamtausgabe),* edited by Friedrich Wilhelm Rust. Rust's edition maintained the original clefs.

---

[6] The publishing firm of Vogt was taken over by Ignaz J. Pleyel in 1802.

[7] Walter Kolneder, *Kunst der Fuge. Mythen des 20. Jahrhunderts,* p. 561.

Along with these new musical editions, a number of analytical treatises on the work appeared in the nineteenth century. These include: *Erläuterungen zu J.S. Bachs 'Kunst der Fuge'* (Commentary on Bach's *The Art of Fugue*) by Moritz Hauptmann (1841); *Bach 'Art of Fugue'* by James Higgs (1877); *Analyse von Bachs 'Kunst der Fuge'* (Analysis of Bach's *The Art of Fugue*) by Hugo Riemann (1894); and *'Die Kunst der Fuge' von J.S. Bach* by Soloman Jadassohn (1895, rev. 1899).

Public awareness of *The Art of Fugue* grew on many overlapping levels during the nineteenth century. On the one hand, interest in Bach and the "strict old style" of composition increased, while, on the other, the demand for piano and organ literature expanded dramatically. The work acquired its reputation as a "formula work" in the nineteenth century, and it was also during this period that it became fully established as a paragon of fugal composition by the advocates of a historically based music pedagogy.

In addition, *The Art of Fugue* was highly prized as an example of contrapuntal mastery in the nineteenth century. Forkel characterized it as an illustrative work which demonstrated "those possibilities which can be constructed out of a [single] fugue subject" (1802). Nägeli was astounded by this "giant work of fugal art" (1826), while Czerny saw the cycle as "an unsurpassed product of harmonic discernment" (1838). Hermann Barth called *The Art of Fugue* a "monument of the strict old style" in all its "architectonic magnificence" (1901), and Philipp Wolfrum praised the cycle as "contrapuntal speculation of staggering proportions" (1906).

In the nineteenth century, the aesthetic value of *The Art of Fugue* was always weighed against its scholarly and pedagogical importance, however. Moritz Hauptman writes that "the musical-poetic soul of this work should be considered secondary [to the study of its contrapuntal techniques]. . . . Its most important tendency is not toward the pure aesthetic but, rather, toward instruction, and for that reason, the great master is nowhere to be recognized here" (1841).

Hugo Riemann went even further: *"The Art of Fugue,* taken as a whole, . . . is actually not an artwork at all, but rather a school work; all aesthetic appeal in the work has been abandoned" (1894). Philipp Spitta, however, had already spoken against this view in his two volume monograph on the life and works of Bach (1880). He argued that *The Art of Fugue* would be misunderstood if "it were considered to be only a set of textbook fugues, instead of a true work of art." Spitta claimed that *The Art of Fugue* "was a composition without peer in both its artistic completeness and its immeasurable depth of emotion." He further claimed that, though the work was certainly "viewed with awe as Bach's last large work," it remained almost entirely foreign to the life of the German people.

Built on Spitta's broader view of the work, furthered by the pioneering spirit of the 1920's and propelled forward by the personal enthusiasm of the young prodigy and Berlin mathematics student, Wolfgang Graeser, a plan emerged to perform *The Art of Fugue* in a large concert hall. In a comprehensive essay entitled *Bachs 'Kunst der Fuge,'* which appeared in the 1924 *Bach Jahrbuch,* Graeser called *The Art of Fugue* one of the purest, most complete embodiments of our (Western) spirit, and "one of the nation's most precious examples of excellence. In this time of subjugation, of inward and outward poverty, the German people should reflect on the historical contributions of its greatest spirits."

After answering numerous attacks on the aesthetic value of *The Art of Fugue,* Graeser managed to bring together the forces for what has been called the premiere performance of the complete cycle. It took place in Leipzig's St. Thomas Church on July 26, 1927, under the musical direction of Karl Straube. This performance featured Graeser's arrangements of the score for string quartet, string orchestra, trumpets, trombones, oboes, bassoons, organ, and harpsichord. Graeser established his own order for the fugues so that the progression of movements would appear to increase in intensity throughout the performance. A glance at Graeser's score indicates that the premiere must have been full of emotional expression. After trumpets and trombones, with their "hard and numbing" sounds finished the closing fugue fragment, the chorale *(Wenn wir in höchsten Nöten sein)* was quietly played by strings and organ.

The effect of *The Art of Fugue* on the Leipzig audience was indeed overwhelming. Alfred Heuss stated that the performance was "perhaps the greatest instrumental event of the entire century." Felix Stössinger claimed that the performance "was a religious service *(Gottesdienst)* in itself," and according to Hugo Löbmann, the name 'BACH' appeared, "like one of the saints."

After its Leipzig premiere, *The Art of Fugue* was suddenly in constant demand as a concert work. Kolneder lists twenty performances in 1928, seventeen performances in 1929, ten performances in 1930, etc. Furthermore, from the time of its premiere to the present, both the work itself and its effect upon the listener have taken on almost supernatural proportions. As a result, *The Art of Fugue* has been described by a bevy of superlatives. Hugo Löbmann spoke about the "gigantic construction of this fugue-world" (1927). Richard Benz claimed that *The Art of Fugue* represents "the mathematics of the cosmos" (1935). Erich Doflein described the cycle as "the most German musical work that can be imagined" (1936), Arnold Schering, as an "enormous cosmic fugue of 2032 measures" (1941), Georg Bieri termed it "a piece [whose motivating idea comes] straight out of the late middle ages" (1950), and Friedrich Blume wrote that *The Art of Fugue* is a "cycloptic torso, left behind as the inheritance of a thousand-year history" (1951). *The Art of Fugue* has been further described by Karl Gustav Fellerer as "the final spiritualization of counterpoint, free from sound, free from words" (1966), and as "a mighty manifestation of the spiritual '*I*'," by Karl F. Wengert (1975).

As *The Art of Fugue* continued to be performed, more and more listeners were astounded by its profound musical qualities. Alban Berg used the words "deepest music" to describe the sense of wonder he experienced during a performance. He wrote to his wife from Zürich in early 1928: "Yesterday, Bach's *Art of Fugue,* magnificent!! . . . [A] work, that hitherto had been considered only 'mathematical,' has been orchestrated by a young German: *deepest music!!"* Nevertheless, there remained a "mathematical," instructive, scholarly, abstract, and artificial side to *The Art of Fugue,* which also shared responsibility for the reverence and awe accorded the cycle. Whether because of the aesthetic effect produced during performances (in spite of its artistically restrained contrapuntal nature) or because it was viewed as an abstract reflection of cosmic order, *The Art of Fugue* took on an ever increasing mystical significance.

Public Performance

Ever since Wolfgang Graeser introduced the music world to a complete performance of *The Art of Fugue,* the question remains as to whether the work should even be performed. Indeed, a major problem remains impossible to resolve, even though the "deepest music" can be experienced during a performance of the cycle; that is, we must face head on the artistically unreconcilable difficulty of transforming Bach's *The Art of Fugue* into a form which the composer never intended.

After the first printing and publication of the work, there might well have been performances of individual movements by small groups of knowledgeable individuals or circles of aficionados, but we know almost nothing about these events. There is little doubt that Bach would have approved such private performances. In any case, there would have been neither opportunity nor place for a complete performance of *The Art of Fugue* before an audience during the time of Bach. According to Werner Breig, the length of the work would have strongly discouraged the mounting of a public performance in the mid-eighteenth century.[8]

Performances of instrumental works (concerti, sonatas, suites) during that time lasted somewhere between fifteen and twenty minutes, whereas a complete performance of *The Art of Fugue* takes nearly ninety minutes. *The Goldberg Variations* lasts approximately forty-five minutes (if the repeats are omitted) and, for that reason, it is also unlikely that they were publicly performed during

---

8 Werner Breig, "Bachs 'Kunst der Fuge': Zur instrumentalen Bestimmung und zum Zyklus-Charakter," *Bach-Jahrbuch* (1982): 103-23.

the time of Bach. As opposed to *The Art of Fugue,* however, *The Goldberg Variations* were definitely written to be rehearsed and performed. In his article, Breig makes a distinction between "a composition cycle" and "a performance cycle." He holds that *The Goldberg Variations* are best considered in the latter category, whereas *The Art of Fugue* belongs to the former.

With the exception of the three-voice mirror fugue, Bach constructed every movement of *The Art of Fugue* so that it could be played on (pedal) harpsichord or organ. Because the inverted double counterpoint of the three-voice mirror fugue is impossible to play on a single instrument, Bach even took the trouble to produce a separate arrangement of this movement for two harpsichords, which was then appended to the cycle. The ability to play materials at the keyboard should not be taken as clear sign that *The Art of Fugue* was composed for performance, however. Playability here could also correspond with a pedagogical intention—that is, what is composed should be playable, and what is composed to be studied should be capable of musical realization by a student.

For the same reason, the two-staff notational format found in the autograph of the closing fugue should not be interpreted too strongly as an indication that *The Art of Fugue* was intended for actual performance.[9] This two-staff notation could just as easily have a pedagogical motivation, since it demonstrates Bach's contrapuntal voice leading in a format that is easy to read at the keyboard. That the individual movements of the work exhibit a high level of artistry also does not guarantee that the work was intended for performance. As Bach understood his role as a composition teacher, any demonstration of contrapuntal processes would have been naturally bound to a high level of musical artistry.

It is not necessary to hear a performance of *The Art of Fugue* in order to understand its overall artistic structure. It is quite possible, by score study alone, to comprehend the elegant way in which the individual contrapuncti are connected to each other, the succession of movements, the axial symmetry of the cycle, and its rhetorical content. Clearly, the characteristics of *The Art of Fugue* do not seem to be primarily those of a performable work, but rather, those of a pedagogical treatise. This observation remains viable, in spite of the fact that the cycle can (and does) stand alone as an artwork, and can indeed be played.

The fact remains, however, that the aspect of playability is subordinate to its major role as a pedagogical discourse and demonstration work. It is as if Bach did not even consider the possibility of public performance when creating this cycle. By this, I do not mean that *The Art of Fugue* should go unperformed today (this is not the point at all!). I mean only that performance tends to transport the

---

[9] Bach's two-stave autograph notation was transcribed into open score for the first printed edition. [Translator's note: See the unbound pages that accompany the Berlin Autograph, labeled *Zum Original Manuscript der 'Kunst der Fuge' von Joh. Seb. Bach/Fünf originale Blätter in Quartfolio* (BWV 1080:19).]

work out of the realm of its original intent. For that reason, performances of *The Art of Fugue* encounter a number of unresolvable difficulties.[10]

To begin with, we shall consider the problem of choosing a performance instrument. Though the piano is the obvious choice for private study, it would not make a particularly good performance instrument for this work, and it is clear that we must base our choice of performance medium, not on how well an instrument functions as a study aid, but on the basis of how suitable it is on stage. Both the organ and the harpsichord are somewhat better suited for a performance of *The Art of Fugue* than the piano, but since the organ (with its many and varied registrational possibilities) can create enormous differentiations in both timbre and dynamic intensity, the harpsichord is, perhaps, a better choice. The harpsichord maintains a relatively even timbre and dynamic level throughout its range, which corresponds more directly to the equally weighted contrapuntal voices in *The Art of Fugue*. In addition, we have already discussed one reason why a stringed keyboard instrument tends to represent the complex contrapuntal texture of the work better.[11] To choose the harpsichord as a performance medium, however, is to create another set of unresolvable difficulties. At the point in a performance where the three-voice mirror fugue is played [in its four-voice arrangement], both a second instrument and a second player are required, which establishes a very unusual [walk-on, walk-off] role for the second performer. Furthermore, a harpsichord performance also faces the difficulty of maintaining audience interest [for ninety minutes], without the help of much idiomatic keyboard figuration or major changes in timbre. As opposed to *The Art of Fugue,* both the *Well-Tempered Clavier* and *The Goldberg Variations* have a much better audience appeal because they contain musical materials which are much more characteristic of keyboard performance practices.

Whether *The Art of Fugue* is played by a large orchestra or by a chamber group, there are a number of practical difficulties that can be overcome in an ensemble performance.[12] In addition, an ensemble performance can also better support and bring to audience attention the characteristic progressive momentum of the cycle as each movement proceeds to the next. It is quite clear, however, that Bach never intended this composition to be orchestrated, much less performed by an instrumental ensemble.

---

[10] The question of performance duration will not be considered a problem in our discussion here, since the maximum length of a performance is judged by completely different standards today than it was in the time of Bach.

[11] See chapter 6, p.65, No.2.

[12] Although Graeser produced his arrangement of the score for performance by a large orchestra, a chamber orchestra is the norm for ensemble performances of the work today.

Any ensemble performance of *The Art of Fugue* presupposes an orchestration of the score, however, and orchestrations inevitably bring with them a high degree of subjective interpretation which unavoidably alters, and can even contradict, the composer's original intentions. For example, it is possible to describe the timbre of every instrument with certain rhetorical characteristics (e.g., the timbre of the oboe can be considered "elegiatic"; the trumpet, "festive"; the trombone, "solemn"). If a particular instrument is assigned to one of the contrapuntal voices in the work, then that voice will be somewhat influenced by the coloristic rhetorical attributes associated with that instrument. Therefore, any instrumentation/orchestration of *The Art of Fugue* will tend to establish a particular set of expressive associations between specific instruments and the lines they play. However, the rhetoric associated with these timbres may not always agree with the fundamental intentions of the materials themselves.

Questions of how to orchestrate specific passages in the cycle can be very complex. For example, should a passus-duriusculus figure, found in combination with suspiratio and quarta falsa, be orchestrated by the "elegiatic" sound of the oboe, the "aggressive" sound of the clarinet, or the "introspective" sound of the violin? In fact, any answer to this kind of question demands an interpretation foreign to the basic nature of the work; that is, the very process of making instrumental assignments modifies, to some extent, the fundamentally important rhetorical statements contained in the materials of the original score. Furthermore, the question of choosing instrumental timbres and establishing levels of dynamic intensity only becomes important when the contrapuncti are transformed into performable pieces.[13] It can be argued that any such transformation actually alienates us from the work's fundamental character.

The arranger must also deal with the inevitable question of whether to orchestrally bring to the foreground or relegate to the background a subject, countersubject or another contrapuntal voice which seems to run counter to the prevailing scope and weight of the other voices. For example, a countervoice which accompanies the entrance of a subject may be just as musically important as the subject itself, [but the arranger may have to choose which one to emphasize]. There are also certain contrapuntal and rhetorical ideas in *The Art of Fugue* which do not lend themselves well to being passed "back-and-forth" between various timbres. Examples are the tied-note motives and contrapuntal-nudge figures in Contrapunctus I or the continual dotted-note rhythms of Contrapunctus II.

There is certainly no reason to forbid ensemble performances of *The Art of Fugue* or, for that matter, further arrangements of the cycle, providing that such

---

[13] There are no indications of orchestrational color or dynamic markings in either the autograph manuscripts or first printed edition of *The Art of Fugue*.

performances and arrangements are recognized to be only imperfect representations of Bach's intentions and that no complete solution to the difficulties encountered in *The Art of Fugue* is possible. Granted, the work is playable, but it was not composed for performance, and all performance arrangements will need to make compromises between conflicting considerations (such as those we have discussed). Certainly, one of the major stimuli for creating new arrangements of *The Art of Fugue* is the challenge of overcoming the problems of previous performance editions through innovative interpretation, but despite the best intentions, it is not even possible to clearly define all of the difficulties that must be overcome.

The fragmented ending of the cycle provides a further unresolvable difficulty for a concert performance. Unlike the problems mentioned above, however, this problem does not arise from attempts to interpret the musical materials of the original score, but, rather, is imposed upon the work by outside considerations [Bach's illness and death]. In spite of its incompleteness, however, the omission of the final fragment from a performance would effectively eliminate both the compositional and rhetorical high-points of the work. For this reason, there have been a number of attempts to complete the fragment, but all of them lack authority.

In many performances, the fragment is played through until, one at a time, the voices break off into silence. This practice, however, produces an inevitable emotional impact which gives rise to thoughts that have nothing to do with the cycle itself. Even a performance of the chorale directly after the end of the fragment does little to mitigate the unrelenting impact of such a sudden breaking off of fugal texture. This point is underscored in a report from the 1928 German Bach Festival in Kassel:

> As the materials of the BACH theme were suddenly broken off by the last note of Bach's overpowering quadruple fugue, the celestially gentle final chorale, *Vor deinen Thron tret ich hiermit,* entered to usher us into the realm of eternity. Audience members stood transfixed, while they listened to the pulsating sounds of painful sadness that hovered over them. There was no sound of applause. Only a foreboding sense of mysticism prevailed, which groped its way, in the shadow of death, after the secretive form of the dead master.

Even if it were possible (for the sake of performance expediency) to attempt other methods of closing off *The Art of Fugue* (a radiant major-key Bach work might be substituted for the chorale, for example), there is no real solution to the problem of its fragmentary ending. Moreover, though an orchestral performance might soften the emotional impact, I am convinced that adding anything to smooth over the abrupt ending of the fragment only adulterates the basic intentions of the work.

Finally, we must consider the general feasibility of *The Art of Fugue* as a concert work. Since I do not want to pass judgement on what music is appropriate for concert audiences and what music is not, I shall refrain from sweeping generalities and speak only for myself. To be completely honest, I must confess that listening to a full concert performance of *The Art of Fugue* somewhat overtaxes me. Why should that be?

I believe that there is no other work of comparable size, not even among the works of Bach, that is so highly concentrated and thickly composed as *The Art of Fugue*. This cycle is so self-contained in the unfolding of its own ideas that it shows little real concern for the exigencies of performance, such as a balance between emotional high and low points, playfulness and seriousness, tension versus relaxation, or a contrast between extroverted and introverted musical gestures.

Certainly, I do not mean that *The Art of Fugue* has value only as an abstract study work, or that it is expressionless or unplayable. My interpretation attempts to prove just the opposite. Nevertheless, it is my view that the expressive content and playability of the work are firmly rooted in its nature as a pedagogical treatise and as a demonstration of contrapuntal art in the medium of fugue. The compositional density of the cycle, which can overtax a listener during a complete performance, does not seem to be intended for an audience at all, but rather for the student of contrapuntal and compositional processes. Furthermore, the musical materials, though playable, were probably not designed so much for public performance as for score study.

The eighteenth century considered Bach's *The Art of Fugue* a practical pedagogical tool for a subject that scarcely anyone was still required to master, while the nineteenth century gave it prominence because musicians began to marvel at the fugal counterpoint it contained (though they did not yet recognize the depth of the music itself). It was only in the twentieth century that the musical profundity of this work began to be recognized. This prompted a separation between the playable nature of the cycle and its function as a demonstration treatise, and thus *The Art of Fugue* was transformed into a performance work.

May *The Art of Fugue* be publicly performed, today and tomorrow, in concert halls and churches; may musicians constantly struggle anew with the unresolvable performance problems of the work, but as far as I am concerned, this music can be perfectly represented only one way—in the understanding which I carry within me.

TOPICAL BIBLIOGRAPHY

Sources

Bach, Johann Sebastian. *Die Kunst der Fuge (BWV 1080): Autograph, Originaldruck.* Faksimile-Reihe Bachscher Werke und Schriftstücke, Herausgegeben von Bach-Archiv Leipzig, Band XIV (Leipzig: VEB Deutscher Verlag für Musik, 1979), Lizenzausgabe B. Schott's Söhne, Mainz.

Schultz, Hans-Joachim. *Dokumente zum Nachwirken Johann Sebastian Bachs 1750-1800.* Assembled from documents held by the Bach-Archive Leipzig, ed. Werner Neumann, supplement to Bach, Johann Sebastian, *Neue Ausgabe sämtlicher Werke,* Band III (Kassel and Leipzig, 1972).

Schmieder, Wolfgang. *Bach-Werke-Verzeichnis* (BWV), sixth ed. (Leipzig, 1976). A systematic-thematic index to the musical works of Johann Sebastian Bach.

Complete Descriptions of the Work

Bergel, Erich. *Johann Sebastian Bach—Die Kunst der Fugue: Ihre geistige Grundlage im Zeichen der thematischen Bipolarität* (Bonn, 1980). This treatise only became known to the author after the completion of the manuscript for this book.

Wolgang Graeser. "Bachs 'Kunst der Fuge'," *Bach-Jahrbuch* (1924): 1-104.

Kolneder, Walter. *Die Kunst der Fuge: Mythen des 20. Jahrhunderts,* 4 vols. (Wilhelmshaven, Taschenbücher zur Musikwissenschaft [vols. 42-45], 1977). Reviews by Alfred Dürr, *Musikforschung* 32 (1979), 153-56; Christoph Wolff, *Musica* 33 (1979): 288f.

Schwebsch, Erich. *Johann Sebastian Bach und die Kunst der Fuge,* second ed. (Kassel, 1955).

The Emergence of the Work

"Bach's 'Art of Fugue': An Examination of the Sources," *Current Musicology* 19 (1975): 47-77.

Wolfgang Wiemer. "Zur Datierung des Erstdrucks der 'Kunst der Fuge'," *Musikforschung* 31 (1978): 181-85.

Christoph Wolff. "Zur Chronologie und Kompositionsgeschichte von Bachs Kunst der Fuge," *Beiträge zur Musikwissenschaft* (1983): 130-42.

The Ground Theme

Hepworth, George. *Das B.A.C.H. in Joh. Seb. Bach's 'Kunst der Fuge,'* (Leipzig, 1887).

Wilhelm Keller. "Das Thema der 'Kunst der Fuge'," *Zeitschrift für Musik* 111 (1950): 71-73.

The Closing Fugue

Gustav Nottebohm. "J.S. Bachs letzte Fuge," *Musikwelt* 1(1880-81): 232-36; 244-46.

Christoph Wolff. "The Last Fugue: Unfinished?," *Current Musicology* 19 (1975): 71-77.

The Chorale

Klotz, Hans. Kritische Bericht zu: Bach, Johann Sebastian. *Neue Ausgabe sämtlicher Werke,* Serie IV, Band 2: *Die Orgelchoräle aus der Leipziger Originalhandschrift* (Kassel, 1957).

Christoph Wolff. "J.S. Bachs 'Sterbechoral': Kritische Fragen an einen Mythos," *Studies in Renaissance and Baroque Music in Honor of Arthur Mendel*, ed. Robert L. Marshall (Kassel, 1974): 283-97.

Williams, Peter. *The Organ Music of J.S. Bach,* vol.2 [works based on Chorales] (Cambridge, 1980).

Determination of Instruments, Arrangement of the Movements, The Cycle and Questions of Symmetry

Werner Breig. "Bachs 'Kunst der Fuge': Zur instrumentalen Bestimmung und zum Zyklus-Charakter," *Bach-Jahrbuch* (1982): 103-23.

Werner Breig. "Bachs Goldberg-Variationen als zyklisches Werk," *Archiv für Musikwissenschaft* 32 (1975): 243-65.

Gregory Butler. "Ordering Problems in J.S. Bach's 'Art of Fugue' Resolved," *Musical Quarterly* 69 (1983): 44-61.

Heinrich Husmann. "Die Kunst der Fuge als Klavierwerk: Besetzung und Anordnung," *Bach-Jahrbuch* (1938): 3-61.

Wiemer, Wolfgang. *Die wiederhergestellte Ordnung in Johann Sebastian Bachs Kunst der Fuge: Untersuchungen am Originaldruck* (Wiesbaden, 1977). Reviews by: Alfred Dürr, *Musikforschung* 32 (1979): 156f; Christoph Wolff, *Musica* 33 (1979): 288f.

Christoph Wolff. "Ordnungsprinzipien in den Originaldrucken Bachscher Werke," *Bach-Interpretationen*, ed. Martin Geck (Göttingen, Kleine Vandenhoeck-Reihe, Band 291, 1969).

Contrapunctus

Klaus-Jürgen Sachs. "Contrapunctus/Kontrapunkt: Begriffsmonographie," *Handwörterbuch der musikalischen Terminologie* (Wiesbaden, 1982).

Musical Rhetoric

Eggebrecht, Hans Heinrich. *Heinrich Schütz: Musicus poeticus,* second ed. (Wilhelmshaven, 1984).

Willibald Gurlitt. "Musik und Rhetorik: Hinweise auf ihre geschichtliche Grundlageneinheit," *Helicon* 5 (1944): 67-86. Reprinted: *Beihefte zum Archiv für Musikwissenschaft*, vol.1 (Wiesbaden,1966): 62-81.

Schmitz, Arnold. *Die Bildlichkeit der wortgebundenen Musik J.S. Bachs,* second ed. (Wilhelmshaven, 1984).

Musical Affections

Dammann, Rolf. *Der Musikbegriff im deutschen Barock,* second ed. (Laaber, 1984).

Numerical Symbols

Ulrich Meyer. "Zum Problem der Zahlen in J.S. Bachs Werk," *Musik und Kirche* 49 (1979): 58-71.

Mitzler's Society for Musical Scholarship

Hoke, Hans Gunter. *Zu Johann Sebastian Bachs 'Die Kunst der Fuge'* (Leipzig, 1979).

Bach's Illness

Helmut Zeraschi. "Bach und der Okulist Taylor," *Bach-Jahrbuch* (1956): 52-64.

INDEX

ABOUT THE AUTHOR

Hans Heinrich Eggebrecht was born in Dresden in 1919. He began formal musical studies in Weimar and then continued the study of musicology, philosophy and Germanistics in Berlin. He received his doctoral degree *(Promotion)* in Jena (1949) and was subsequently granted tenured professorship *(Habilitation)* in Freiburg (1955). He has taught at a number of important German universities (Berlin, Erlangen and Heidelberg), and since 1961 has held the position of Professor of Musicology at the University of Freiburg. One of his most significant accomplishments is the writing of the section on musical terms as well as other topics of historical importance for the twelfth edition of Riemann's *Musik Lexikon.* Among Eggebrecht's most important other published works are: *Studien zur musikalischen Terminologie* (1955); *Heinrich Schütz: Musicus poeticus* (1959); *Die Orgelbewegung* (1967); *Beethoven und der Begriff der Klassik* (1971); *Versuch über die Wiener Klassik* (1972); *Zur Geschichte der Beethoven-Rezeption: Beethoven 1970* (1972); *Musikalisches Denken* (1977); *Sinn und Gehalt* (1979); and *Die Musik Gustav Mahlers* (1982).

ABOUT THE TRANSLATOR

Jeffrey Prater is a member of the music faculty at Iowa State University, where he is Associate Professor of Music and Chair of the Music Theory Division. Born in Endicott, New York, he received a Ph.D. in Music Composition from the University of Iowa, a Master of Music degree from Michigan State University, and his baccalaureate degree from Iowa State University. Among his teachers are William Bergsma, Richard Hervig, H. Owen Reed and Gary White. Before coming to Iowa State University, he held faculty positions at the University of Wisconsin Center-Marinette and Northern Michigan University.

Dr. Prater pursues a strong interest in musical analysis, analysis for the performing musician, and the history and pedagogy of music theory. He has regularly presented lectures and papers at professional meetings, and has written an acclaimed article on "The Great War's Effect on Schönberg's Development of the Twelve-Tone Method" *(College Music Symposium, 1986)*. He has also been active as a reviewer of music textbooks and scholarly works. As a composer, Prater has written and published works in a variety of genres and has been the recipient of numerous grants, awards and commissions for composition.

During the 1988-89 academic year, Prater received a faculty improvement leave from Iowa State University. He spent his leave time in northern Germany, where he began the translation of this and another book on music theory.

DATE DUE